EASY GOURMET COOKING
FOR YOUNG PEOPLE AND BEGINNERS

EASY GOURMET COOKING

FOR YOUNG PEOPLE AND BEGINNERS

BY BERNICE KOHN
ILLUSTRATED BY TONY APILADO

The Bobbs-Merrill Company, Inc.
Indianapolis   New York

The author is grateful to Danielle Panter, twelve-year-old research
assistant extraordinary, whose kitchen testing of many of these
recipes was of immeasurable help.

THE BOBBS-MERRILL COMPANY, INC.
Publishers   Indianapolis   New York

Copyright © 1973 by Bernice Kohn
Design by Tony Apilado
Printed in the United States of America
All rights reserved
ISBN 0-672-51701-9
Library of Congress catalog card number 73–1752
0 9 8 7 6 5 4 3 2

This book is dedicated with love and gratitude to my husband, Morton, who proved that *anyone* can be a gourmet cook!

CONTENTS

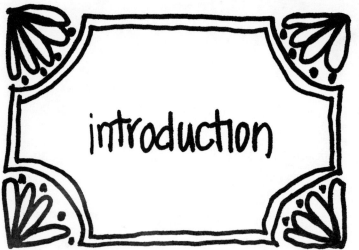

introduction

This is a very special cookbook. It is for the beginning cook who has never made anything more complicated than scrambled eggs. It is for the young cook who doesn't know the difference between a spatula and a colander—and doesn't care. It is for the lazy cook who hates to spend an hour (or even a minute) cleaning up the kitchen. And yet, it is for the artist cook who truly loves to create, who, lazy or not, can't settle for opening a can or package of something-or-other and letting it go at that. It is for anyone at all who wants to cook really good food in very little time. Its motto is 1-2-3 gourmet!

If you show these recipes to your Great-aunt Matilda, she'll sneer: You *can't* make a decent cake without sifting flour; a rich, delectable sauce can*not* be produced in ten seconds; it is impossible to make tender, crumbly brownies in five minutes and have only one pan, one cup and a spoon to wash; and besides, it takes years of experience to make the kinds of things listed in the index.

Great-aunt Matilda is wrong. You can prove it yourself. If you can read, you can make everything in this cookbook. You won't need any equipment that can't be found in most kitchens. With a few exceptions, there are no strange ingredients called for—although the end product is often thoroughly exotic. All of the recipes are easy. All of them are good. Some of them are great because they take advantage of shortcuts that Auntie never dreamed of. And unless you are plagued with bad luck, they will all work!

All of these recipes were developed by trial and error. There were a number of failures, to be sure. What remains are the successes. A modest number of them, perhaps, but enough—if you combine them cleverly—to provide you with at least one hundred good, workable, easy gourmet menus.

More important than the recipes is the concept: forget the old bugaboos. Be daring. Your purist cookbook may say that you have to sift the flour three times and clarify the butter; maybe you do—then again, maybe you don't. Try it and see. It's the only way you'll ever find out.

But until you are ready to be experimental, you are fairly safe with this collection. It has been tried by everyone from a twelve-year-old girl to my own husband, whose culinary skills were formerly confined to the barbecue.

Before you begin, just a few general rules:

No food is better than the quality of its ingredients. Don't cheat. When the recipe calls for butter, use butter. Vanilla always means pure vanilla extract, not imitation vanilla flavoring.

Don't change the recipe—at least not the first time. All good cooks develop their own "style," and you will too. Change and improvise to your heart's content (that's how all of these recipes came into being) but only *after* you have learned the basic method.

If you love to cook but hate to clean up (doesn't everybody?), think twice before you use another bowl, plate, or spoon. All of the recipes here are planned for maximum dishwashing economy. When you are left in the lurch for something to put the nuts or the raisins in, use a paper towel, a paper napkin, or the table top.

Wherever vanilla is called for, the directions tell you to measure it in the bottle cap. Doesn't it matter whether you have a small bottle or a large bottle? Not really. Conventional cookbooks usually say "1 teaspoonful of vanilla." I have found it to be a totally non-critical measurement. A little more, a little less, it just doesn't matter.

The same rule (or lack of rule) applies to measurements like "⅛ teaspoon." *Please* don't waste time measuring ⅛ teaspoon of anything. Use a dash, a pinch, a sprinkle. It will be just fine.

When we get into larger quantities—spoonfuls, cupfuls, and the like—be a little more careful. The measurements mean a *level* spoonful, or a *level* cupful. But again, you don't have to spend minutes carefully leveling off the top of the spoon with a knife. Unless you're measuring dynamite, just make sure it *looks* level, not rounded or heaped up.

Many of the recipes call for chopped nuts (because I love nuts). You may wish to buy them already chopped. If you don't, the easiest way to do it yourself is in a blender. If you don't have a blender, you may have a nut grinder or a wooden chopping bowl and knife. Lacking all of these things, chop a few nuts at a time with the blade of a large sharp knife against a cutting board.

To separate an egg, tap the egg sharply on the edge of a cup. Pull the shell apart slowly and carefully so that the egg white dribbles out into the cup and the yolk stays in one half of the shell. If you have never separated an egg before and the yolk accidentally falls into the cup, do your best to fish it out with half a shell or a spoon. Or if it seems easier, hold back the yolk with a spoon and pour off the white into something else.

Pans are most easily buttered with your fingers. If greasy fingers bother you, use a scrap of paper towel or the paper the butter was wrapped in. In any case, if you do it first and set the pans aside, you can wash your hands and have done with it.

One final note about baking at high altitude: Raise the baking temperature 25° F. And, oh yes, at any altitude, if you use glass baking pans for cakes, *lower* the oven temperature 25° F from the one you would normally use.

CAKES & PIES

CAKE

First things first. I have wasted countless hours of my life leafing frantically through cookbooks looking for some gorgeous, gooey goody to make for dessert. This time, cakes and pies are where they belong, right up front. See? You've saved time already.

Since everything in this book is backwards, let's start right off with what most cooks (wrongly) consider one of the most difficult productions, a rich, buttery cake. This is a 1–2–3 all-purpose recipe and enough to give you a reputation as a pastry chef if you never bake again. It makes a chocolate layer cake—or a coconut or vanilla one, or any other kind. It can become a birthday cake, a strawberry shortcake, a nut-loaf cake, or a large batch of cupcakes.

For some reason or other, people seem to be impressed (if not absolutely overcome) when they find out that you didn't use a mix but made the cake "from scratch." Here, then, is the scratch:

BERNICE'S BASIC CAKE

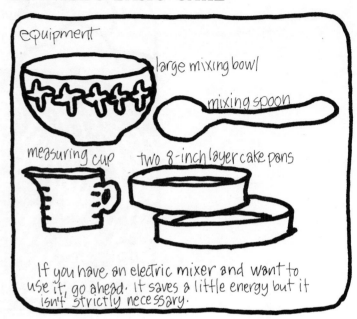

equipment

large mixing bowl

mixing spoon

measuring cup

two 8-inch layer cake pans

If you have an electric mixer and want to use it, go ahead. It saves a little energy but it isn't strictly necessary.

INGREDIENTS

½ cup (¼ pound or 1 stick) butter, at room temperature

1 cup sugar

2 eggs

1¾ cups self-rising cake flour (You can find this in any market. It has the baking powder and salt already added to the flour and is a good time-saver.)

1 cup milk

1 capful vanilla

PROCEDURE

1. Take the butter out of the refrigerator as soon as you get the inspiration to bake. It *must* be soft.

2. Turn on the oven at 350° F.

3. Butter the baking pans with a thin film of butter and set them aside.

4. Put the ½ cup butter into the bowl and mash it with a spoon (or mixer) until it is creamy and smooth.

5. Add sugar and beat until mixture is fluffy.

6. Crack the two eggs (one at a time) on the edge of the bowl, pull the two halves of shell apart and let the egg fall into the bowl. If a scrap of shell falls in, pick it out. Beat the eggs into the butter and sugar until the mixture looks light, smooth, and free of lumps.

7. Add the capful of vanilla.

8. Up to this point, there has been no particular reason to hurry. You might even have answered the phone—but from here on, don't. You are about to add the self-rising flour and that means strictly business until the cake is in the oven. A cake is light and fluffy because as soon as baking powder gets wet, it begins to give off a gas that fills the batter with little bubbles. If you don't get the cake into the oven promptly after you add the baking powder, the gas will rise through the batter all right—only it will continue to rise right out the top and into the air. Instead of a fluffy cake, you might wind up with a heavy pancake.

   This warning is not meant to throw you into a panic, but just to make sure that you're fairly well organized. So take a look at the oven temperature and see if it's right. If it isn't, fix it. OK? Now. Add the self-rising cake flour.

9. Fill the measuring cup (without washing it) with one cup of milk and pour about half of it into the bowl. Stir quickly with the spoon until the flour is all wet. Now beat for a minute or two, scraping the sides of the bowl often. When the batter is smooth and fluffy, add the rest of the milk and beat a little more. Don't beat for more than 3 minutes altogether. Far more cakes are ruined by overbeating than by underbeating. Remember those gas bubbles.

10. Divide the batter equally into the two pans.

11. Pick up each pan with both hands and give it a couple of hard taps on the table. This will break any large air bubbles that got trapped when you poured the batter.

12. Put the pans into the oven and do *not* open the door for the first fifteen minutes.

13. Cakes should not be jarred while they are baking. Be careful about slamming the oven door. If your oven has a glass door and you don't have to open it, so much the better. If the door is solid, take a

peek after fifteen minutes and see what's happening. If the oven is not level and the cakes are getting lopsided, turn them around quickly but gently.

14. The cakes should be done in about 25–30 minutes, but oven temperatures are rarely accurate enough to allow you to bake just by the clock. You will have to look. A cake is done when it is golden brown and has begun to pull away from the sides of the pan. Press your finger lightly on the top of the cake. It should feel spongy and pop back when you take your finger away. If you don't think you can tell that way, stick a toothpick into the center of the cake and see if it comes out clean. If the toothpick is covered with goo, the cake is not done.

15. Remove the pans from the oven and set them on wire racks, trivets, the range top, or anything that will let air circulate underneath. Let the cakes remain in the pans until cool to the touch.

16. Put one cake on a plate and cover it with a filling. You can use jam, whipped cream, or any sliced fruit. Put the other layer on top and cover it with whipped cream or any of the frostings in the next chapter. You can also use the frostings as a filling between the layers as well. Directions for frosting a cake are on p. 13.

VARIATIONS

Use nine-inch layer pans for a larger, flatter cake. Or, use one nine-by-nine-inch square pan, a nine-by-twelve-inch rectangular one, a loaf pan, tube pan, or muffin tins for cupcakes. The baking time will be somewhat different for each kind of pan. Start checking cupcakes after 15 minutes, a loaf cake after 25. It may take 40 minutes —or more—to get done.

Add a handful of chopped nuts or raisins to loaf cake batter just before you put it into the pan.

When you prefer a simple cake, omit the frosting and either sprinkle the top with confectioner's sugar or leave it entirely plain.

PIE

Did you ever try to make a pie and wind up with pastry dough stuck to your board, rolling-pin, hands, and hair? And, as a reward for your trouble, a sad, raggy-looking piece of gook full of holes? It *is* possible to roll pastry smoothly and neatly—but it rarely seems as easy as some people would have you believe. Here are some good ways out.

GALETTE FRUIT PIE

Don't let that fancy name frighten you. It's French, it looks and tastes French—but you don't have to be French to make it.

equipment for pastry

middle-size mixing bowl

measuring cup

tablespoon

teaspoon

9-inch pie pan

INGREDIENTS FOR GALETTE PASTRY

1 cup flour
1 tablespoon sugar
½ teaspoon salt
6 tablespoons (¾ stick) butter at room temperature
1 egg yolk
1 tablespoon water
1½ tablespoons lemon juice

PROCEDURE

1. Put out butter to soften.
2. Turn on oven at 425° F.
3. Put flour, sugar, and salt into the bowl.
4. Add the soft butter.
5. Add the egg yolk to the bowl.
6. Add the water and the lemon juice.
7. Mix it all together with a spoon and then with your fingertips until it is well blended.
8. Take the pastry out of the bowl and put it into the center of the unbuttered pie pan. Now, with your fingertips, press gently and work the pastry out to the sides of the pan. If you make holes, patch them up. Keep pressing the pastry right up the sides of the pan until it comes to the top. Use your thumb to make "dimples" all around the rim to form a scalloped edge.

FILLING

You can use any kind of fruit for filling galette pastry and the method remains about the same. Two particularly good fruits to use, when they are in season, are peaches and plums. Here are the directions for

PLUM FILLING

equipment
cutting board
sharp knife
measuring cup
tablespoon
small saucepan

INGREDIENTS

about 10–15 ripe plums, depending on size
1 tablespoon sugar (use a little more if the plums are very sour)
1 tablespoon lemon juice
½ cup currant jelly for glaze (optional)

PROCEDURE

1. Wash the plums under cold water and cut them in half. Discard the seeds.

2. Arrange the fruit in the pastry in an attractive fashion. One good way is to place the plum halves in slightly overlapping circles beginning at the outside of the circle and working in toward the center. Put the cut sides down, skin side up. When the arrangement is just right, sprinkle the sugar and lemon juice evenly over the top of the fruit.

3. Put the pie into the heated oven and bake it for 30 minutes.

4. If you have decided to use the glaze (and you should), prepare it as soon as the pie is out of the oven. Empty the currant jelly into a small saucepan and melt it over very low heat. Stir it often so that it doesn't burn. As soon as the jelly is melted, pour it evenly over the hot pie. It will set as it cools. The pie can be served cold or when it is just slightly warm.

NUTTY PEACH PIE

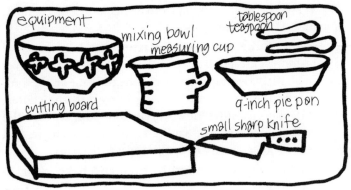

equipment
mixing bowl
tablespoon
teaspoon
measuring cup
cutting board
9-inch pie pan
small sharp knife

INGREDIENTS

Crust

½ cup finely chopped, unsalted walnuts or almonds
1 cup flour
¼ teaspoon (a pinch) salt
5 tablespoons butter, room temperature (½ stick plus
    1 tablespoon)
1 teaspoon water

Filling

6 to 8 ripe peaches
½ cup sugar
1 tablespoon flour (in addition to the 1 cup)
sprinkle of cinnamon
sprinkle of nutmeg
1 egg
½ cup milk

PROCEDURE

1. Put the chopped nuts, salt, 1 cup of flour, butter, and water into the bowl.

2. Mix everything together with your fingertips until it is thoroughly blended.

3. Put the mixture into the center of the pie pan and press it evenly over the bottom and up the sides to the rim.

4. Turn on the oven to 450° F.

5. Wash the peaches under cold water and slice them into ½-inch slices on the cutting board. As you slice the peaches, put them into the same bowl (unwashed, of course) you used for the nut crust mixture.

6. Add the sugar, 1 tablespoonful of flour, a sprinkle each of cinnamon and nutmeg. Mix with a spoon.

7. Spread the peaches into the pie shell.

8. In the same bowl (still unwashed), beat one egg with a spoon and add ½ cup of milk.

9. Drizzle the mixture all over the top of the peaches and then put the pie into the oven.

10. Bake it for 10 minutes at 450° F, then lower the temperature to 350° and bake it for 30 minutes more. Cool completely. It's good just as is, sensational with vanilla ice cream.

You can make the same Nutty Pie Crust but instead of filling it with peaches, use it for cream pie.

CREAM PIE

The filling for this one is chocolate, vanilla, or butter-scotch pudding. Buy your favorite flavor and prepare it according to the directions on the package. Just be sure you get the kind that has to be cooked, not an "instant" pudding.

1. Turn on the oven to 350° F.
2. Follow steps 1, 2, and 3 in the Nutty Peach Pie recipe.
3. Bake the empty pie crust for 30–35 minutes, or until it just begins to turn golden brown around the edges.
4. While the pie crust is cooling, prepare the pudding.
5. Cool the pudding slightly, then pour it into the crust. When it is thoroughly cool, put it into the refrigerator.
6. Just before serving, heap whipped cream (see page 16) over the top.

CRUMBY PIE

This crust can be made with graham crackers or zwieback, or chocolate or vanilla cookies—even corn flakes. You don't have to bake it.

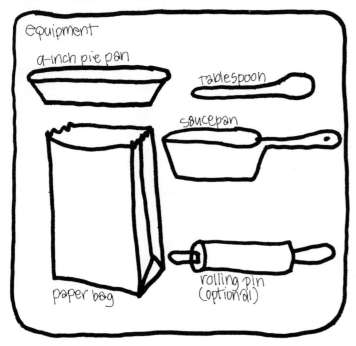

1. Put the butter into a saucepan and melt it over very low heat. Turn off heat at once.

2. Put the zwieback, crackers, cookies, or flakes into a paper bag and crush them by rolling the bag with a rolling pin. If you don't have a rolling pin, use a jar, bottle, vase, baseball bat, or anything that rolls.

3. Pour the finely crushed crumbs into the pan of melted butter.

4. Add the sugar, using a little less than 4 tablespoons if you made your crumbs with very sweet cookies.

5. Mix well with a spoon.

6. Put all but about 1/2 cup of the mixture into the pie pan and use your fingers to press it evenly over the bottom and up the sides. Save the extra crumb mixture to sprinkle over the top of the pie when it is all finished.

7. Put the pan in the refrigerator and chill it for two hours or longer.

8. Fill the crust with pudding and whipped cream as in the Cream Pie recipe that precedes this one.

INGREDIENTS

enough cookies, crackers or whatever to make about 2
   cups of crumbs
1/4 pound (1 stick) butter
4 tablespoons sugar

SHIFTY CHIFFON

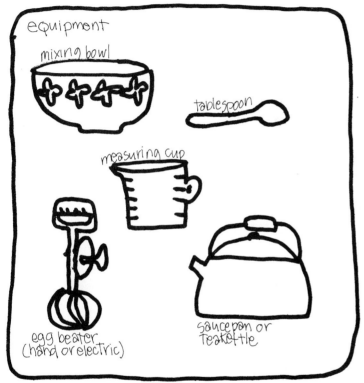

equipment

mixing bowl

tablespoon

measuring cup

egg beater
(hand or electric)

saucepan or
teakettle

INGREDIENTS

1 Crumby Pie crust (opposite)
1 cup boiling water
1 package fruit gelatin—raspberry, strawberry, cherry,
    or your own favorite flavor
1½ cups (¾ pint) vanilla ice cream

PROCEDURE

1. Ignore the directions on the gelatin package. Pour the gelatin and 1 cup of boiling water into a bowl and stir until gelatin is completely dissolved.

2. Let the mixture cool, then put it into the refrigerator. When it just begins to thicken—like glue—but before it has really set—take it out again.

3. Remove the ice cream from the freezer and break it into chunks with a spoon. Leave it out while you

4. Beat the gelatin with an eggbeater until it is light-colored and frothy.

5. Add the ice cream and continue to beat until the entire mixture is well blended and very fluffy.

6. Pile it into the prepared piecrust and refrigerate until serving time (allowing at least a couple of hours for it to set).

FROSTINGS

Now that you are an experienced baker of cakes and pies, you'll need a few toppings for them.

HOW TO FROST A CAKE

Put the cake (which *must* be cool before you start) on a plate and spread the frosting over the top and sides with a flat-bladed knife or a spatula. If it's a layer cake, use the same frosting between the layers—or substitute raspberry or apricot jam instead. You can make the frosting on top of the cake rough and swirly and peaky by playing sculptor with the knife blade. If you prefer a smooth finish, keep a cup or glass of very hot water handy. Dip the knife blade into it frequently and gloss over the frosting until it is glassy smooth. This is also a good way to make emergency repairs if the frosting begins to set and gets messy in spots.

When you are all finished, dampen a paper towel and wipe the edges of the plate clean. If you like, you can decorate the top of the cake with nuts, little candies, sprinkles, or what-have-you.

CHOCOLATE BUTTER CREAM FROSTING

equipment

saucepan

spoon

measuring cup

eggbeater (hand or electric)

INGREDIENTS (for a 2-layer cake)

5 ounces (squares) unsweetened cooking chocolate
¼ pound (1 stick) butter
2½ cups confectioner's sugar (also called 10-x sugar)
a few grains of salt
½ capful vanilla
a few spoonfuls milk or cream

PROCEDURE

1. Put the butter and chocolate into the saucepan and melt them both together over very, very low heat, stirring frequently.

2. Cool slightly, then add the confectioner's sugar, salt, and vanilla. Stir all together with a spoon as well as you can.

3. Add a spoonful of milk (or cream) and stir again. If the mixture is still too thick to stir, add a tiny bit more milk, then a tiny, tiny bit more. The object is to make the frosting *just* loose enough to make it possible to beat it. You have to be very careful at this point, because if you add too much liquid the frosting will become runny. If such a catastrophe does befall you, don't despair. You can thicken it all up again by adding some more sugar—but the frosting will be better if that doesn't happen.

4. As soon as it is possible to get a beater going, do so. Use a hand beater, an electric one, or just a big spoon. In any case, beat until there are no lumps at all.

VANILLA (AND OTHER) BUTTER CREAM FROSTING

equipment

medium-size bowl

tablespoon

measuring cup

INGREDIENTS (for one layer; double recipe to use between layers)

¼ cup (½ stick) butter, room temperature
1 cup confectioner's (10-x) sugar
1 egg yolk
½ capful vanilla

PROCEDURE

Put everything into the bowl at once and beat with a spoon until perfectly smooth. If the egg yolk was small and the mixture is too hard to beat, add a few drops (from a teaspoon) of milk or water.

VARIATIONS

Add a couple of spoonfuls of crushed strawberries, bananas, raspberries, well-drained canned, crushed pineapple, grated lemon or orange peel, chopped nuts, chocolate chips, crushed nut brittle, or jam. If you use a fresh fruit that makes the frosting too runny, add a little more confectioner's sugar to make it thick again.

WHIPPED CREAM

For strawberry shortcake (or banana or any other kind), and for all those luscious cream pies.

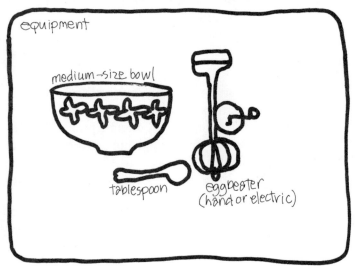

INGREDIENTS

1 small container (½ pint, or 1 cup) heavy cream
½ tablespoon sugar
1 capful vanilla

PROCEDURE

1. If the weather is very hot, chill the bowl and beater before you start. In ordinary weather this is not necessary, but do be sure that the cream is very cold.

2. Put the cream into the bowl and beat hard and fast until it is as thick as melted ice cream. Every once in a while, stir the cream from the sides of the bowl into the center.

3. Add the sugar and vanilla, and now beat rather slowly and stir often. If you beat too much, you will make butter instead of whipped cream.

4. As soon as the cream begins to look thick, test it every few seconds by lifting the beater to see if you can make the cream stand up in a little peak. As soon as you can, it's done.

5. Give the whipped cream a few hard stirs with a spoon and cover the bowl and refrigerate it unless you are going to use it at once. Whipped cream can remain in the refrigerator for several hours if necessary. If you do have to store it, beat it for a few seconds with a spoon before serving.

COOKIES

Everybody likes cookies. Not everybody, however, likes to bake them, because they are often too much trouble. These cookies—like the other things in this book—are all shortcut cookies. Even though the recipes are easy, there are a few general hints that will keep you from running into snags.

Many cookies burn easily. If you have a timer, use it. If you don't, watch the clock. Since oven temperatures are not always accurate, it is a good idea to check all cookies a few minutes before they are supposed to be finished. If the edges are very brown, make sure you rescue them before they turn black.

The recipes here are each for about three dozen cookies and will make more than one panful. If you have two cookie pans, use them both at the same time. If not, all of the cookie doughs can safely be left in the bowl while the first batch is baking. Since the baking time is short, you won't have too long a delay.

Some of the recipes call for brown sugar. Try to get the free-pouring kind since it is easy to measure.

Unless the recipe specifically tells you not to butter the pan, butter it lightly *each* time you use it.

And just one more thing. Conventional cookbooks always talk about "drop" cookies and lead you to believe that the dough just drops off the end of a spoon. It doesn't. You have to push it off with your finger. We won't talk about "drop" cookies—but any time the recipe talks about putting dough on the pan by the spoonful, be prepared to give it a shove.

HEAVENLY BROWNIES

These brownies are complete unto themselves, but for a special dessert, serve them à la mode with vanilla ice cream.

equipment

medium-size saucepan

spoon

measuring cup

8x8-inch square pan
(you can use a 9x9 pan, too,
but the brownies won't be as thick)

INGREDIENTS

6 tablespoons (¾ stick) butter
2½ ounces (squares) unsweetened baking chocolate
1 cup sugar
2 eggs
1 capful vanilla
½ cup (or just a handful) shelled pecans or walnuts
⅔ cup self-rising cake flour

PROCEDURE

1. Turn on oven at 350° F.
2. Butter pan.
3. Put butter and chocolate into saucepan and set over *very* low heat. Stir constantly until chocolate is all melted. If it starts to stick to the bottom, lift the pan off the stove and continue to stir.
4. Set the melted chocolate and butter aside to cool. While you are waiting, break up the nuts with your fingers. They should not be finely chopped.
5. When the chocolate mixture is cool enough to stick your finger into, add 1 cup of sugar and stir.
6. Add 2 eggs and beat with the spoon until smooth.
7. Add vanilla.
8. Add the self-rising flour and stir until the flour disappears.
9. Stir in the nuts.
10. Spoon the mixture into the pan. It will be very thick, so smooth it out somewhat with the back of the spoon. It will smooth more as it bakes.
11. Bake for about 25 minutes—or until the brownies feel fairly solid when you touch them quickly with a fingertip. This makes very gooey, fudgey brownies which I think are the best. If you like the drier kind, bake a little longer until the batter begins to shrink from the sides of the pan.
12. Let the brownies cool in the pan, then cut them into squares.

ALMOND COCOONS

These are, without question, the most popular of *my* cookie repertory among my family and friends. I have named them *Cocoons* because I have found the cocoon shape the quickest and easiest to make. If you feel like being more ambitious, shape them in the classic Viennese tradition and call them Almond Crescents.

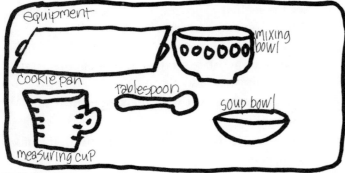

INGREDIENTS

1 cup (½ pound or 2 sticks) butter, room temperature
5 tablespoons granulated sugar
2 cups flour
1 cup ground or finely chopped almonds
1 cup confectioner's (10-x) sugar with 2 capfuls vanilla
    well mixed into it

   (If you are going to make these cookies often, prepare vanilla sugar the professional way. Buy a vanilla bean, break it into ½-inch pieces, and put them into a closed jar of confectioner's sugar. After a few days the vanilla flavor will be absorbed by the sugar.)

PROCEDURE

1. Put all of the ingredients—except the confectioner's sugar—into the mixing bowl and mix with your fingertips until everything is well blended.

2. Turn on the oven to 325° F and butter the cookie pan very lightly.

3. Take a small handful of dough and roll it into a thin sausage, the way children make clay "snakes." Break off pieces half the size of your first finger and shape them neatly into either cocoons or crescents. Place them on the cookie pan so that they are close together but not quite touching. They spread only slightly as they bake.

4. Bake for 20–30 minutes. The cookies must not turn brown. They should just begin to show a faint golden tinge near the bottom.

5. Take the cookies out of the oven. While they are still warm (but not hot), roll each one in a soup bowl of vanilla confectioner's sugar, then set it aside on a tray or counter top to cool. When the cookies are cold, store them in an airtight tin. They will keep well for several weeks, so they can be made in advance for gifts.

BROWN LACE COOKIES

do not keep for weeks. They are at their best when they are freshly made.

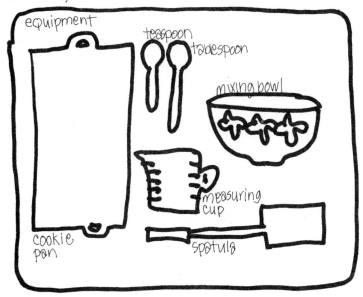

INGREDIENTS

4 tablespoons (½ stick) butter, room temperature
2 cups brown sugar (free-pouring)
2 eggs
½ cup flour
½ cup finely chopped pecans (you may substitute walnuts or almonds)
1 teaspoon baking powder
1 capful vanilla

PROCEDURE

1. Turn on oven at 400° F.
2. Mix the butter and sugar together in a bowl until they are well blended.
3. Stir in the eggs.
4. Add the flour, baking powder, and nuts and blend well.
5. Rub a little butter over the bottom of the pan and place the cookie mixture on it by the half-teaspoonful. Leave 3 inches between blobs because they will spread into large, very thin wafers as they bake.
6. Bake for about 5–7 minutes. Watch *very* closely because the thin edges burn easily.
7. Remove the cookies from the oven and let them cool for a few minutes. It is impossible to handle them while they are hot since they are very soft. As soon as they get hard enough to hold their shape, remove them from the pan with a spatula and spread them on a counter or table top until they are cold. Store them in a covered tin or other airtight container.

CHOCOLATE COOKIES

equipment
saucepan
measuring cup
cookie pan
tablespoon

Ingredients

2 ounces (squares) unsweetened chocolate
1/4 pound (1 stick) butter
2/3 cup brown sugar
1/3 cup white sugar
1 egg
1 1/2 cups flour
small pinch salt
capful of vanilla

Procedure

1. Put the chocolate into the saucepan and melt it over the lowest heat possible, stirring constantly.

2. As soon as the chocolate has melted, remove the pan from the stove and add the butter.

3. Fill the measuring cup to the 2/3 mark with brown sugar, then add white sugar until the 1-cup mark is reached. Add the sugar to the saucepan and stir until the butter is melted and all of the ingredients are blended.

4. Turn on the oven at 350° F and butter the cookie pan.

5. Break an egg into the saucepan and stir it around a bit. Add all the rest of the ingredients and stir until the flour disappears.

6. With your hands, form the dough into little balls the size of oversized marbles. (If you have ever played jacks, aim for the size of a jacks ball.)

7. Flatten each ball between your palms so that it is about the size of a half-dollar coin and about 1/4 inch (more or less) thick. Place the cookies on the pan, not quite touching but fairly close together. They will spread very little. Place a pecan half (or some other nutmeat) or a few chocolate sprinkles on top of each cookie.

8. Bake for 12 minutes. You can let the cookies cool right in the pan if you want to. They won't stick. If you have to use the pan again, you can remove the cookies while warm and spread them out to cool. Be sure to butter the pan again before you use it.

PEANUT BUTTER COOKIES

INGREDIENTS

½ cup (1 stick) butter, room temperature
½ cup crunchy (chunk-style) peanut butter
½ cup brown sugar
1 egg
1¼ cups flour
pinch salt
¼ teaspoon baking powder
¼ teaspoon baking soda
½ capful vanilla

PROCEDURE

1. Heat oven to 350° F.

2. Mix butter and peanut butter together with a spoon in the mixing bowl.

3. Fill the measuring cup to the ½ mark with white sugar, then to the 1-cup mark with brown sugar. Pour the cupful of combined sugars into the bowl and mix.

4. Add all of the other ingredients and stir until thoroughly blended.

5. Roll pieces of dough between your palms to make balls halfway between the size of marbles and that of Ping-Pong balls. Place them 1 inch apart on an ungreased cookie pan.

6. With a fork, make a crisscross in the top of each cookie, pressing it into a round shape as you do so.

7. Bake 10–15 minutes or until very lightly browned. Cool in pan or remove while warm.

CHOCOLATE CHIP COOKIES

equipment

cookie pan

measuring cup

mixing bowl

teaspoon
tablespoon

spatula

1. Turn on oven at 350° F.
2. Butter the cookie pan.
3. Mix the butter and both sugars in the bowl until well blended.
4. Add everything else and mix until you can't see any flour.
5. Put the dough on the pan by the teaspoonful. Leave about 2 inches between spoonfuls since the cookies spread while baking.
6. Bake for about 12 minutes or until the cookies begin to brown around the edges. Remove them from the tins onto a flat surface. Store when cold.

INGREDIENTS

½ cup (1 stick) butter, room temperature
½ cup brown sugar
¼ cup white sugar
1 egg
½ teaspoon baking soda
1 teaspoon water
1 cup flour
½ cup chopped nuts
1 package (6 ounces) chocolate bits

QUICK BREADS

Every standard cookbook has recipes for various kinds of yeast breads. While there is nothing better than a good loaf of homemade bread, yeast bread does not fit the 1–2–3 gourmet image. It takes too long. Here, then, are some breads that are quick and easy.

CORN BREAD

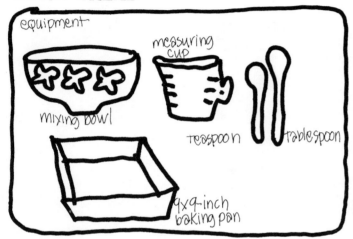

INGREDIENTS

1¼ cups corn meal
¼ cup flour
2 tablespoons sugar
3 teaspoons baking powder
1 teaspoon salt
1 egg
1 cup plus 2 tablespoons milk
3 tablespoons soft butter

PROCEDURE

1. Set oven to 425° F.

2. Butter pan, bottom and sides.

3. Put corn meal, flour, sugar, baking powder and salt into a mixing bowl and stir together.

4. Add the egg, milk, and butter, and beat with a spoon. As soon as all the big lumps are gone (the batter will never be really smooth because corn meal is grainy), pour it into the pan.

5. Bake for 20–25 minutes or until the top begins to turn golden brown.

WHEAT GERM BISCUITS

Biscuits are a popular form of quick bread, but they usually have to be rolled and cut into circles. You can skip both steps with these.

equipment

Cookie pan

mixing bowl

teaspoon

tablespoon

measuring cup

INGREDIENTS

1½ cups flour
½ cup wheat germ
1 tablespoon baking powder
1 teaspoon salt
¼ cup peanut oil (or other pure vegetable oil—except olive oil)
¾ cup milk

PROCEDURE

1. Set oven to 450° F.
2. Rub a small amount of oil over bottom of pan.
3. Put flour, wheat germ, baking powder, and salt into bowl and mix with a spoon.
4. Add the milk and oil and stir until mixture is well blended.
5. With your hands, form the dough into balls the size of golf balls and place them on the pan about 1 inch apart. Press down the tops very, very gently, just enough to flatten the balls slightly.
6. Bake for 10–12 minutes or until biscuits begin to turn golden.

CREAM CHEESE BISCUITS

are subtitled Idiot Biscuits. If you can't make them, give up cooking.

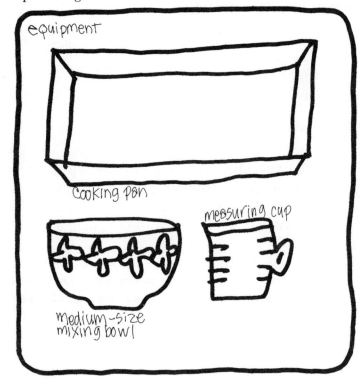

equipment

cooking pan

measuring cup

medium-size mixing bowl

INGREDIENTS

½ cup (1 stick) butter, room temperature
3-ounce package cream cheese, room temperature
1 cup flour

1. Set oven to 350° F.
2. Put all of the ingredients into the bowl and knead them together with your fingers.
3. Shape the dough into golf balls and set them on the pan.
4. Flatten the tops, just enough to make them look like biscuits instead of balls.
5. Put the pan into the oven and bake for 12–15 minutes or until the biscuits are golden brown.

DATE NUT MUFFINS

If you like a sweet bread for breakfast or for afternoon tea, try these.

equipment
muffin pan that holds 8 large or 12 small muffins
mixing bowl
measuring cup
teaspoon
tablespoon

INGREDIENTS

2 cups flour
2 tablespoons sugar
1 tablespoon baking powder
½ teaspoon salt
½ cup chopped walnuts or pecans
10 dates, pitted and cut into small pieces
½ cup milk
½ cup orange juice
1 egg
¼ cup peanut or corn oil

PROCEDURE

1. Set oven to 425° F.
2. Grease bottom and sides of each cup of muffin pan with oil.
3. Put the flour, sugar, baking powder, salt, nuts and dates into the mixing bowl.
4. Add the milk, orange juice, egg, and oil.
5. Stir until the flour is completely moistened and the egg is well blended, but do not beat. The mixture will be lumpy because of the dates and nuts.
6. Spoon the batter into the muffin cups, making each one about ⅔ full.
7. Bake for 25 minutes or until each muffin is brown on top and around the edges.

APPETIZERS

CRUDITÉES WITH BLUE CHEESE DIP

Cruditées is the French word for raw vegetables. Use radishes, tiny tomatoes, celery sticks, scallions, broccoli or cauliflower florets, tender young asparagus. Heap all the vegetables together in a bowl with ice cubes. To make the dip:

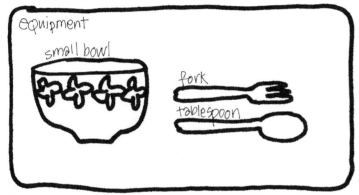

INGREDIENTS

1 small container sour cream
3 tablespoons blue cheese

PROCEDURE

1. Put the blue cheese into a bowl and mash it with a fork.
2. Beat in the sour cream.
3. Refrigerate until serving time.

GUACAMOLE

is another "light-weight" dip to serve with corn chips or potato chips.

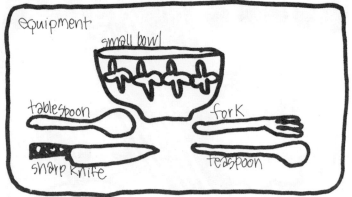

INGREDIENTS

1 ripe avocado
2 tablespoons tomato cut into tiny pieces
1 teaspoon very finely chopped onion
salt and pepper
juice of ½ lemon

PROCEDURE

1. Peel the avocado. Cut it into pieces and mash it with a fork in a bowl.

2. Sprinkle the lemon juice over the avocado and mash it some more, until it is quite smooth.

3. Mix in tomato, onion, and salt and pepper to taste.

VARIATION

Instead of serving guacamole as a dip, you can put a mound of it on a lettuce leaf and serve it as a first course or a salad.

CHOPPED CHICKEN LIVERS

equipment
skillet
small knife
small saucepan with cover
wooden chopping bowl with chopping knife
fork

INGREDIENTS

½ pound chicken livers
2 to 3 tablespoons butter
2 hard-boiled eggs
small onion
mayonnaise
salt and pepper

PROCEDURE

1. To make hard-boiled eggs, put the raw eggs into the saucepan. Cover them with cold water and put them on the stove over medium heat. When the water comes to a boil, turn the heat low, cover the pan, and boil for 10 minutes. Remove the eggs from the stove at once and stand them under cold running water for a few minutes. Eggs that are cooled quickly are easy to peel.

2. While you are waiting for the eggs to cook, melt the butter in the skillet over medium heat and add the livers. Cook them for about 10 minutes, turning them several times with a fork. Do not allow the livers to become brown or crisp around the edges. They are done when you cut one in half with a fork and the inside is the same color as the outside and the texture is tender but not gooey.

3. Peel the eggs and put them into the chopping bowl with the chicken livers and a slice of raw onion about the size of a silver dollar.

4. Chop it all with a chopping knife until the grains are smaller than rice.

5. Add a heaping forkful of mayonnaise and a sprinkle of salt and pepper. Mix with the fork. The mayonnaise should just hold the mixture together in a smooth paste. If it is still crumbly, add more mayonnaise. Taste to see if it needs more salt and pepper. If you are planning to serve it on salty crackers, add a little less salt than you would otherwise.

6. Keep it chilled in the refrigerator until serving time. Serve on a lettuce leaf as a first course, or as a spread on crackers, small slices of thin toast, or thin slices of black bread.

PERFECT PICKLES

are perfect for an unusual appetizer—or meal accompaniment—or between-meal snack.

The most common pickles are made with cucumbers. There's nothing wrong with cucumber pickles, of course, but the fact is, you can pickle almost any vegetable. An assortment of pickles not only is delicious, it's a thing of beauty as well. Use young cucumbers cut into slices, quarters or thin spears; whole raw green beans; green tomatoes cut into quarters or eighths; small sections of cauliflower or broccoli flowers; small raw zucchini squash cut into spears; strips of carrot or celery. Make one vegetable at a time, or combine any or all of them in the same jar.

equipment!

saucepan that holds one quart or more

measuring cup

Two one-quart size jars with tight-fitting screw caps. Preserving jars are best, but if you don't have them use any jars with wide mouths such as mayonnaise jars.

teaspoon

sharp knife

INGREDIENTS

vegetables (you will have to guess at the quantity that will fill the jars)
1 cup white vinegar
2 cups water
¼ cup salt
½ teaspoon dill seed
½ teaspoon mustard seed
2 peeled cloves of garlic (a clove of garlic is one of the small sections of a head of garlic)
2 sprigs of dill (fresh if possible)

PROCEDURE

1. Wash the jars and covers thoroughly with very hot water and soap. Rinse well and set aside.

2. Put into the saucepan the vinegar, water, salt, dill seed, and mustard seed.

3. Wash the vegetables thoroughly in cold water. Do not peel anything except the carrots. Try to get cucumbers that do not have waxed skins. If you can't, peel those, too.

4. Cut the vegetables to the proper sizes.

5. Arrange the vegetables by hand in the jars. If you are using only stringbeans, spears, or strips, stand them on end and pack them as tightly as possible. If you are using slices, or flowers, or a combination of all, pack them as well as you can. Fill the jars to the top.

6. Put the saucepan on the stove and bring the contents to a bubbling boil. Pour it at once into the filled jars, bringing the liquid right up to the top. Make sure that the seeds are evenly divided.

7. Put one clove of garlic and a sprig of dill into each jar and put the lid on as tightly as you can.

8. Turn the jars upside for a few minutes to make the liquid travel around. Watch to see if the lids leak. If they do, open them and put a couple of layers of waxed paper over the tops of the jars, then screw the lids back.

9. Leave the pickles alone for three or four days before you open them. After opening, keep the pickles in the refrigerator.

CROQUE MONSIEUR

Unlike the preceding appetizers, this one is rather hearty. You can cut it into small squares to use as an appetizer or hors d'oeuvre—or serve it whole (one to a person) with salad for a good lunch. It's something like ham and Swiss on French toast.

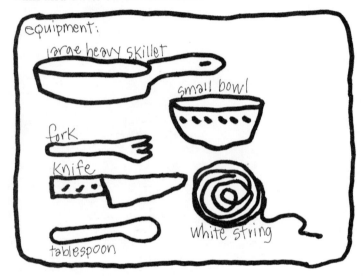

INGREDIENTS (to make 4)

8 slices bread
4 slices boiled or baked ham
4 slices Swiss cheese
2 eggs
1 tablespoon water
4 tablespoons (½ stick) butter

PROCEDURE

1. Melt the butter in the skillet and dip each slice of bread into it quickly to lightly butter one side.

2. Butter side in, make 4 ham and cheese sandwiches.

3. Trim the crusts off the sandwiches (optional), then tie each one with string, in both directions, the way you tie a package.

4. Break the eggs into a small bowl, add about a tablespoonful of water, and beat lightly with a fork.

5. Heat the melted butter that is still in the skillet until it begins to sizzle, then turn the heat very low.

6. Dip each sandwich into the beaten egg, coating both sides thoroughly. Lift it out of the egg with the fork and put it into the skillet. Cook all four sandwiches at once.

7. Cook the croques about 10 minutes on each side, or until they are golden brown.

8. Remove the string before serving.

BIG WHEEL CANAPÉS

are a party in themselves. You don't need another thing except something to drink.

If you have any artistic talents at all, these canapés will win you fame and fortune. They require skill in assemblage and design and really none at all in cooking.

equipment.
a large sharp knife
a collection of small bowls, spoons, forks and knives

INGREDIENTS

a round loaf of pumpernickel bread
the rest is impossible to list—you'll get the idea as you go.

PROCEDURE

1. The first thing you need is a bakery with a round pumpernickel and a bread-slicing machine. Tell the clerk to put the bread into the machine standing up on its side so that the slices come out in big rounds, like this:

You can count on a few puzzled looks, but just pretend you don't notice. If your bakery doesn't have a machine, you'll have to cut the bread the same way with a knife. Try to keep the slices thin and even.

2. Now. The basic step in making the first wheel is to coat one big, round slice of bread with some kind of soft spread. Use soft cream cheese, mayonnaise, or sour cream.

3. After you have slathered on a good coating of something, start at the outside edge of the wheel and make a thin ring of either parsley, watercress, slivers of green pepper, strips of pimiento, or slices of black, green or stuffed olives.

4. Now put something round right in the center of the wheel—a slice of tomato, a slice of hard-boiled egg, a round blob of caviar (red or black), a piece of ham or smoked salmon, or a circle of bologna, salami, or liverwurst.

5. Make a little ring of peppers, olives, or something around the center circle, then fill in the space that's left with egg salad, tuna salad, ham salad, anchovies, crumbled crisp bacon, tomatoes, turkey—anything or everything. The finished wheel will look like this:

6. Very carefully, with a large, sharp knife, cut the wheel in half, into quarters and then into eighths. You will now have eight canapés that look like this:

If you put different ingredients on each wheel, you will wind up with a glittering array of very professional-looking tidbits.

A word of caution is in order here. Even though these are a good exercise in imagination, don't get so carried away by the beauty of it all that the food combinations on any one wheel are not edible. For example, dill pickles and strawberry jam would make a colorful splash—but you probably wouldn't like the taste.

Some good combinations are:
cream cheese, olives, caviar, green pepper, pimiento; mayonnaise, watercress, shrimp or tuna, olives, tomato; mayonnaise, egg salad, crisp bacon, tomato, parsley; mayonnaise, ham, pickles, bits of Swiss cheese; sour cream, caviar, hard egg slices, any kind of smoked fish.

Since the small end slices of the bread aren't worth using, you can figure on about forty-eight canapés from each loaf of pumpernickel.

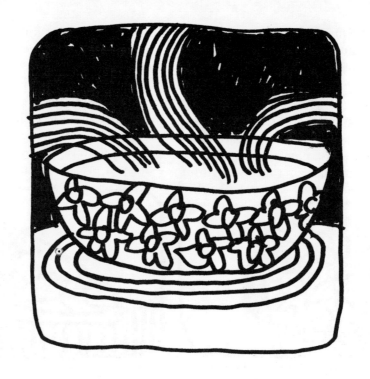

SOUPS

GREEK LEMON SOUP

Soups exist in an almost infinite variety. But, none of your run-of-the-mill standard items here. These are all a little special—and, of course, fast and easy. This one is called *Avgolemono* in Greek.

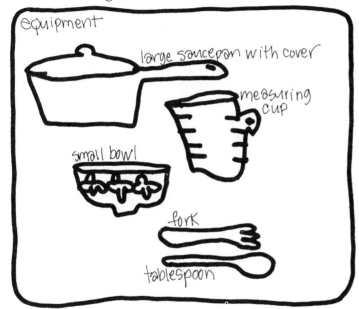

INGREDIENTS (for 6 servings)

2 quarts (8 cups) good quality canned chicken broth
2 eggs
½ cup raw rice
juice of ½ lemon
salt and pepper

1. Bring the soup to a boil in the saucepan. Add the rice and boil gently, covered, until the rice is tender (note cooking time on rice box).

2. Beat the eggs well with a fork in the bowl.

3. Add the lemon juice to the eggs and beat again.

4. A few spoonfuls at a time, add some of the hot soup to the eggs, beating each time. If you don't do this very slowly, the hot soup will cook the eggs and make lumps. When you have added as much soup as will fit into the bowl, pour the mixture into the soup pot. Add salt and pepper to taste, stir vigorously, and serve.

SOPA DE PESCADO ANDALUSIA

This is a typical fish soup of southern Spain.

equipment
a heavy (porcelain, if possible)
soup kettle or large pan
small sharp knife
stirring spoon
teaspoon
measuring cup

INGREDIENTS (to serve 4)

4 slices, about ½ inch thick, French or Italian bread
olive oil
1 medium onion
1 medium green pepper
1 small tomato
1 clove garlic, chopped (optional)
8 cups water
1 pound filet of cod (or halibut or other meaty white fish), cut into 1-inch cubes
a few large raw shrimps, peeled
a few well-scrubbed mussels and cherrystone clams (optional)
½ teaspoon saffron
1 teaspoon salt
pepper
fresh parsley

PROCEDURE

1. Pour a little olive oil into the bottom of the kettle and fry the bread in it until it is golden toasted on both sides. Remove the bread and set aside.

2. Peel and chop the onion and green pepper (coarsely) and add them to the olive oil with the garlic if you use any. Over medium heat, stirring frequently, cook the vegetables until they begin to wilt and the onions are transparent. Do not let them brown. Add more oil if necessary to keep the vegetables from burning. Now chop up the tomato, stir it into the mixture and cook about 5 minutes more.

3. Add the water, salt, pepper, and crumbled-up saffron, and bring to a rolling boil.

4. Put in the fish and the shrimps.

5. Cover and boil gently for about 7 minutes.

6. If you are using shellfish, add them and cook for a few minutes more, just until the shells have opened.

7. Break up the fried bread and add it to the soup. Taste it and add as much more salt as it needs.

8. Toss a handful of coarsely cut-up parsley over the top and serve at once.

FRENCH ONION SOUP

equipment

a heatproof crock or casserole that can go under the broiler as well as on top of the stove.

cutting board

sharp knife

tablespoon

INGREDIENTS (to serve 4–6)

4 to 6 medium-size onions
4 tablespoons (½ stick) butter
2 cans condensed beef consommé or bouillon, diluted
     with water according to directions on the can
salt and pepper
4 slices French or Italian bread
grated Italian cheese

PROCEDURE

1. Peel the onions and slice them as thinly as possible. Sorry about your tears. There's no help for it, so just be brave.

2. Melt the butter in the crock on top of the stove and cook the onions in it until they are golden, transparent, and tender, but not brown. You will have to stir them often.

3. Add the consommé (with necessary water), cover and cook slowly for ½ hour. Taste and add salt and pepper as needed.

4. Turn on the broiler and put the four slices of bread under the flame to toast on one side only. This takes only about a minute, so watch *carefully* or you will make charcoal.

5. Float the bread, toasted side down, in the soup. Sprinkle grated cheese generously over the bread. Put the whole works under the broiler for a few minutes until the cheese melts, the bread toasts and the soup looks good enough to eat.

CREAM OF WALNUT (OR ALMOND OR HAZELNUT) SOUP

This soup is a guaranteed sensation-creator!

equipment

medium-size saucepan

cup

INGREDIENTS (for 4 servings)

½ cup ground or finely chopped walnuts (or almonds or hazelnuts)

1 can condensed chicken broth with 1 can water

½ container (¼ pint or ½ cup) heavy cream

salt and pepper

PROCEDURE

1. Put the chicken broth and water into the pan and bring to a boil.

2. Add the nuts, the cream, and salt and pepper to taste.

3. Heat the soup slowly until it is piping hot but do *not* let it boil again.

44

CREAM OF SPINACH SOUP

is just as good cold as it is hot.

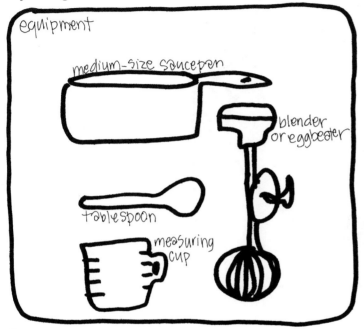

equipment

medium-size saucepan

tablespoon

blender or eggbeater

measuring cup

INGREDIENTS

1 pound fresh spinach if you have a blender, or 1 package frozen chopped spinach if you don't have a blender

1 can condensed chicken broth with ½ can of water

½ cup milk

1 container yogurt (plain) or sour cream

salt and pepper

PROCEDURE

1. Put the spinach into the pan with the soup and water.

2. Bring it to a boil and cook gently for about 3 minutes.

3. If you use fresh spinach and blender: cool the spinach and soup slightly, then put them into the blender with the milk. Blend for 5 seconds.

4. If you use frozen spinach, pour the milk right into the pan and beat the mixture with an eggbeater.

5. Taste the soup and add salt and pepper as needed.

6. To serve hot, heat *without boiling*. To serve cold, refrigerate until icy. Either way, serve the soup with a big blob of yogurt or sour cream floating in each bowl.

EGGS

CREAMY EGGS

Since eggs are something that you can almost always find around the house, it's invaluable to know a few good things to do with them when you need emergency rations.

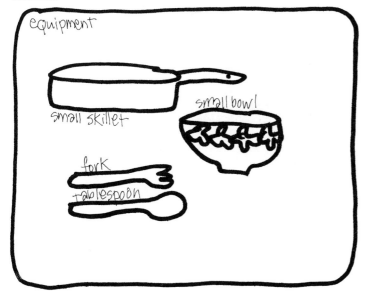

1. Put the cream cheese into the bowl and mash it with a fork.

2. Break the eggs over the cheese, add the water, and beat with the fork until blended.

3. Melt the butter in the skillet. As soon as it begins to sizzle, add the egg mixture. Keep stirring with the fork until the eggs have just barely lost their runniness but are still quite soft. Remove from the stove at once. Add salt and pepper to taste.

INGREDIENTS (to serve 2)

4 eggs
2 tablespoons water
half of a 3-ounce package of cream cheese, room temperature
about ½ tablespoon butter
salt and pepper

OMELETTE AUX FINES HERBES

A classic French luncheon dish.

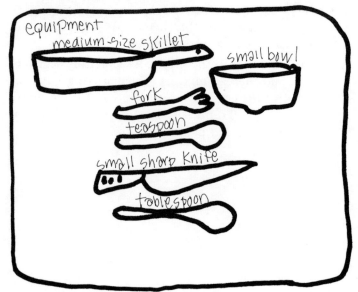

equipment
medium-size skillet
small bowl
fork
teaspoon
small sharp knife
tablespoon

INGREDIENTS (for 2 persons)

4 eggs
1 tablespoon water
½ teaspoon salt
1 tablespoon butter
1 tablespoon finely cut chives (you may use frozen or
    freeze-dried chives)
1 tablespoon finely cut parsley
Optional—a sprinkle of tarragon, thyme, or basil—or
    all three

PROCEDURE

1. Break eggs into bowl, add water and beat lightly
   with a fork.

2. Add the salt and herbs.

3. Melt the butter in the skillet. When it shows the
   first signs of turning brown, add the eggs and stir
   with a spoon. Keep stirring until the eggs have just
   set and you can't see any more liquid. Stop stirring
   and cook a minute or so more, shaking the pan over
   the heat.

4. Remove from the stove. Quickly fold the omelet in
   thirds—first one side toward the center, then the
   other side over it—and slide it onto a serving dish.

CURRIED DEVILED EGGS

are a gourmet variation on an old theme.

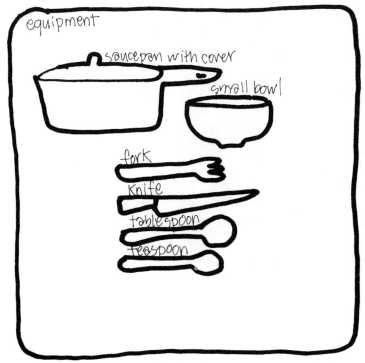

equipment
saucepan with cover
small bowl
fork
knife
tablespoon
teaspoon

INGREDIENTS (to serve 2 for lunch or 4 as an appetizer)

4 eggs
2 tablespoons mayonnaise
¼ teaspoon salt
dash pepper
1 teaspoon curry powder

PROCEDURE

1. Hard-boil the eggs by starting them in cold water and boiling them, covered, for 10 minutes. Set the pan under cold running water to cool the eggs quickly, then peel them.

2. Slice the eggs in half the long way and scoop out the yolks carefully with a teaspoon. Put them into a bowl.

3. Mash the egg yolks with a fork, add all the other ingredients and mix. Taste to see if there is enough salt.

4. If the mixture does not stick together well, add a little more mayonnaise. Beat it with a fork until it becomes quite fluffy.

5. Pile the yolk mixture very lightly into the egg whites and serve them on lettuce leaves or surrounded by sprigs of watercress. Sprinkle the top of each egg with a little paprika or chopped parsley (or both), or decorate each one with a slice of stuffed olive or a caper.

CHOCK
FULL OF CHEESE

FONDUE PUDDING

gives the illusion of being a tricky soufflé. Glamorous as it looks, it's foolproof.

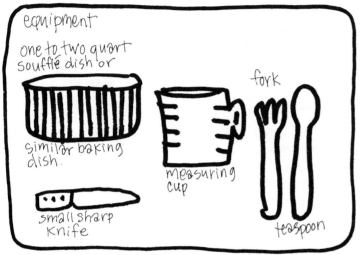

equipment

one to two quart soufflé dish or similar baking dish.

measuring cup

small sharp knife

fork

teaspoon

INGREDIENTS

½ pound Swiss cheese
6 slices French or Italian bread, thickly buttered
3 eggs
1 cup milk
½ teaspoon salt
dash of pepper

PROCEDURE

1. Turn on oven at 325° F.
2. Butter the bottom and sides of the baking dish. Break the eggs into it and beat them lightly with a fork.
3. Cut the buttered bread into 1-inch squares and chop the cheese into little pieces.
4. Add the milk, bread, cheese, and seasonings to the eggs and mix well.
5. Bake for 45 minutes to 1 hour or until the top of the pudding is brown and bubbly. Variations in time will occur, depending on the size and shape of the dish.

QUICHE

Here is the famous French cheese pie in a version as easy as it is extraordinary. Serve it as an elegant luncheon or supper dish (a green salad makes it complete), or cut it into slender wedges and use it as a special-occasion first course or appetizer. If you are in a hurry, you can use a frozen piecrust. It is much better if you make your own.

Pastry

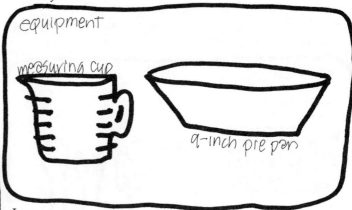

equipment

measuring cup

9-inch pie pan

INGREDIENTS

¼ pound butter (1 stick) at room temperature
a small package (3 ounces) cream cheese at room temperature
1 cup flour
dash salt

PROCEDURE

1. Put all of the ingredients into the pie pan and mix them together with your fingertips.

2. When the mixture is thoroughly blended, press it evenly over the bottom and up the sides of the pan.

3. Leave a rather thick edge at the top and make scallops in it by pressing your thumb all around the rim. Set it aside and make the filling.

Filling

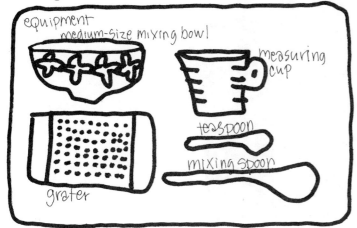

equipment
medium-size mixing bowl
measuring cup
teaspoon
mixing spoon
grater

INGREDIENTS

½ pound Swiss cheese (imported, if possible)

3 eggs

1½ cups milk or cream

½ teaspoon salt

sprinkle of pepper (freshly ground is best)

¼ pound sliced, cooked ham, shredded

     or

8 slices crisply fried bacon, crumbled

     or

1 can crab meat, well drained

     or

1 cup slightly cooked spinach that has been
    well drained and chopped with a
    small slice of onion

} use any *one* of these four things

PROCEDURE

1. Preheat oven to 375° F.
2. Grate the cheese right into the bowl.
3. Add all the other ingredients and beat with a spoon until well blended.
4. Pour the mixture into the waiting pastry shell.
5. Bake for about 45 minutes or until the mixture is not runny in the center. Test it by sticking a table knife into the middle of the quiche. If it is "set," like custard, it's finished. If the center is puddly, bake it a little longer and test again.

FISH & SEAFOOD

SOLE MEUNIÈRE

One of the easiest of all fish dishes to prepare is this classic of French restaurant menus.

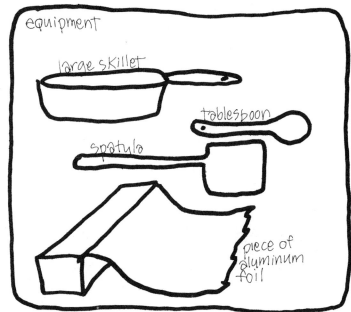

equipment
large skillet
tablespoon
spatula
piece of aluminum foil

INGREDIENTS (to serve 4)

4 portion-size filets of sole (this recipe works with other kinds of fish filets, too)
about 4 or 5 tablespoons flour
4 tablespoons butter
1 lemon
2 tablespoons chopped parsley
salt and pepper

PROCEDURE

1. Put the flour on a sheet of aluminum foil and dip the fish into it, coating both sides. Shake off excess flour.

2. Melt the butter in the skillet over medium heat and heat it until it begins to bubble and shows just the first tinge of brown.

3. Cook the fish for a few minutes on each side, until it is golden brown and an edge flakes apart when you break it with the edge of the spatula.

4. Lift the filets gently onto the serving platter. They are very fragile, so if you have two spatulas, you might find it easier to use them both.

5. To the leftover butter in the pan (plus whatever crumbs of fish that remain) quickly add the juice of a lemon and salt and pepper to taste. Bring to a boil. Pour the sauce over the fish, sprinkle it with chopped parsley and serve immediately.

VARIATION

Some slivered almonds toasted in the pan for a minute before you add the lemon juice turns this into Sole Meunière Amandine.

SUPER SECRET FISH

Even if you don't usually like fish particularly, you will probably love this recipe. It's a very useful people-astounder because it seems to have an impossibly complex sauce. If you can keep the secret, you can go on astounding people with it for years.

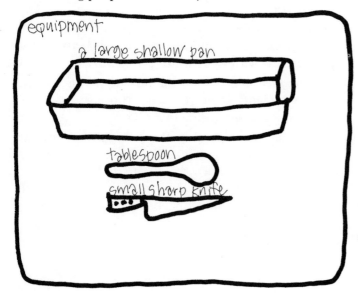

equipment
a large shallow pan
tablespoon
small sharp knife

INGREDIENTS

fish filets of almost any kind. Use bluefish, flounder, fluke, whatever is running that day
good quality mayonnaise (*not* salad dressing)
1 lemon
enough butter to grease the baking pan

PROCEDURE

1. Turn on broiler.
2. Butter the baking pan.
3. Arrange the fish on the pan, skin side down, and spread the top of each filet thickly with mayonnaise.
4. Sprinkle some lemon juice over all.
5. Put the pan under the broiler and broil for about 10 minutes, more or less, depending on the thickness of the fish. You can tell when it's done by breaking off a little piece of fish with a fork. The fish should be flaky and the sauce dark brown and bubbly.

It doesn't need another thing—but if you like, sprinkle some chopped parsley, slivered almonds or sliced olives over the top.

BROILED SHRIMP

can be used as either a main course or an appetizer. As an entrée, a pound of shrimps will serve 2 to 3 people.

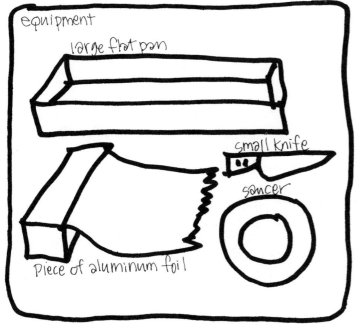

equipment
large flat pan
small knife
saucer
piece of aluminum foil

INGREDIENTS

1 pound large raw shrimps
a saucerful of milk
about 1 cup bread crumbs
garlic powder
salt and pepper
butter (about 3 to 4 tablespoonfuls)

PROCEDURE

1. Turn on the broiler.
2. Peel the shrimps by breaking off the tails and stripping away the shells.
3. Wash the shrimps under cold running water.
4. Pour the crumbs onto a piece of foil.
5. Dip each shrimp in milk and then roll it in crumbs until it is well coated.
6. Lightly butter a baking pan and place the shrimps on it.
7. Cut little dots of butter and put several on top of each shrimp.
8. Sprinkle the whole lot with a little salt, pepper, and garlic powder.
9. Put the pan under the broiler for about 5 minutes, or until the shrimps are golden brown.

TUNA (OR SALMON) CASSEROLE

This is a good item to have in your bag of tricks for an emergency meal. Since the ingredients are things you are likely to have on hand most of the time, you can toss this together when there are unexpected guests—or when it's raining and you don't feel like shopping.

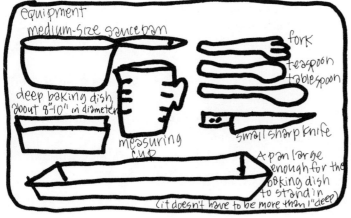

equipment
medium-size saucepan
fork
teaspoon
tablespoon
deep baking dish, about 8"–10" in diameter
measuring cup
small sharp knife
A pan large enough for the baking dish to stand in (it doesn't have to be more than 1" deep)

INGREDIENTS

2 cans tuna fish (or salmon—with the skin and bones taken out), drained
1½ cups milk
1 cup bread crumbs
3 tablespoons butter
2 eggs
½ teaspoon salt
sprinkle of pepper
handful of chopped parsley or celery—or both

PROCEDURE

1. Set oven to 350° F.

2. Put the milk in the saucepan and bring it to a boil. Watch it carefully and turn off the heat as soon as it boils, before it has a chance to boil right out of the pan.

3. Butter the sides and bottom of the baking dish. Melt the rest of the butter by dropping it into the hot milk.

4. Stir the bread crumbs and the fish into the milk mixture. Break up the lumps in the fish with a fork so that it is in smallish flakes.

5. Stir in the eggs, seasonings, and greens, and mix thoroughly.

6. Pour the mixture into the baking dish. Stand the dish in the pan with about an inch of hot water in the bottom of the pan. Put it into the oven and bake it for 1 hour.

7. Serve the casserole with lemon wedges and with or without a white or cheese sauce. (See pages 87–88.)

CHICKEN & DUCK

FOILED CHICKEN

Chicken is great. Everybody likes it and it lends itself to a multitude of variations.

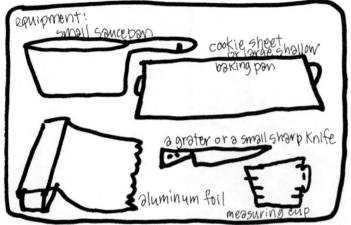

equipment:
small saucepan
cookie sheet or large shallow baking pan
a grater or a small sharp knife
aluminum foil
measuring cup

INGREDIENTS (to serve 4)

3 whole chicken breasts, split and skinned (by the butcher, of course), which is another way of saying 6 *half* breasts

¼ pound (1 stick) butter

1 cup bread crumbs

¼ cup grated (you can buy it that way in a jar) Parmesan cheese

¼ cup Swiss cheese, coarsely grated or chopped into tiny bits with a knife

salt and pepper

7 pieces of aluminum foil, each one large enough to wrap up 1 piece of chicken

PROCEDURE

1. Turn on oven at 450° F.

2. Melt the butter in the saucepan over very low heat.

3. Pour the bread crumbs and both kinds of grated cheese onto a piece of foil (didn't you wonder why it said 7?) and mix well with your fingers.

4. Now stick those crumby fingers into the melted butter and very lightly grease one side of the other 6 pieces of foil.

5. Dip each piece of chicken into the melted butter, shake it off over the pot, sprinkle it with a little salt and pepper, then coat it on both sides with the crumb-cheese mixture.

6. As you finish coating each piece of chicken, put it on the buttered side of a piece of foil and wrap one side over the other, then turn up the ends to make a tight package.

7. Put all the foiled chicken on an ungreased pan and bake it for 30 minutes.

8. Serve it right in the foil if you want to. For more formality, unwrap it onto a platter and put a thin slice of lemon and a sprinkle of chopped parsley on top of each piece.

THE CHICKEN SECRET WEAPON

This is one of those great things that you can make hours (or a day) ahead of time and just heat up at the last minute. In fact it's even better when made in advance since the flavors have more time to blend.

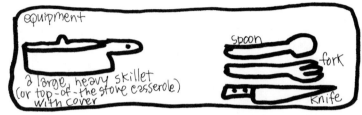

equipment

a large, heavy skillet (or top-of-the-stove casserole) with cover

spoon
fork
knife

INGREDIENTS

1 medium to large chicken, cut into pieces
3 fresh medium-size tomatoes washed and sliced, or 1 small can tomatoes or tomato sauce
dried crushed basil leaves
salt and pepper
olive oil
1 large onion (or 2 small ones), sliced
1 clove garlic, chopped, or a sprinkle of garlic powder (optional)

PROCEDURE

1. Put the pan on the stove over medium heat.

2. Pour a small amount of olive oil into the pan and spread it around with a spoon. Use just enough oil to coat the bottom of the pan with a thin film.

3. Touch a piece of chicken to the oil. When it sizzles, it's hot enough. Put all the chicken (skin side down) and the onions into the pan.

4. Sprinkle the chicken with salt and pepper and basil. Use the basil freely so that the chicken is well dotted with it—like green freckles.

5. Raise some of the chicken with a fork in a few minutes and take a peek at the underside. When it is golden brown, turn it all over and sprinkle it again with salt, pepper, and basil. If the pan looks dry when you turn the chicken, add a little more oil.

6. When the second side of the chicken is brown, add the tomatoes. If you use fresh tomatoes, wash and slice them.

7. Cover the pan tightly and turn the heat as low as it will go. Let the chicken cook for about 45 minutes, or until it is so tender it almost falls off the bones when you move it with a fork. During the cooking time, stir the chicken around occasionally to make sure it doesn't stick on the bottom and to get it all equally coated with sauce.

8. If the sauce seems to be drying up, add a little more tomato or ¼ cup water—or better yet, a splash of dry red wine if you happen to have some open. If you do use wine, be sure to let it cook for at least ten minutes to give the alcohol a chance to boil off.

OVER-FRIED CHICKEN

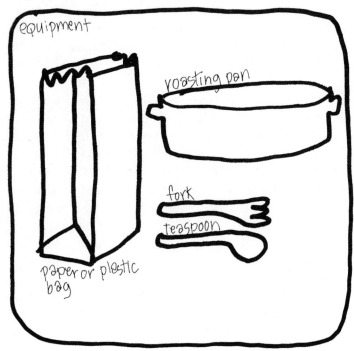

equipment

roasting pan

fork

teaspoon

paper or plastic bag

INGREDIENTS (to serve 4)

1 large cut-up chicken—or 1 or 2 chicken parts per person
1 cup flour
1 teaspoon salt
¼ teaspoon pepper
pure vegetable or peanut oil
about ¼ stick butter (2 tablespoons)

PROCEDURE

1. Put the flour, salt, and pepper into the bag and shake it until it is well mixed.

2. Turn on the oven at 350° F.

3. Put the roasting pan on top of the stove and pour in just enough oil to cover the bottom thinly—about ¼ inch deep. Heat the oil for a minute or two, then turn off the heat.

4. One piece at a time, drop the chicken into the flour bag and, clutching the top of the bag shut, shake it until the chicken is completely coated with flour.

5. Put all the pieces of chicken into the warm oil in a single layer and put the pan into the oven. Bake it until the bottom of the chicken is very brown—about 20 minutes.

6. Turn the chicken with a fork. Put little dots of butter all over the top of every piece and bake it until the bottom is brown—about 25 minutes more. Stick the chicken with a fork to make sure that it's very tender. If it isn't, keep it in the oven (turning again if necessary) until it is.

ROAST DUCK AUX FRUITS FLAMBÉ

This is one of the sneakiest ones of all. Crunchy, crisp roast duck, luscious with rich fruit sauce and flaming with brandy, is usually associated with posh French restaurants and is not often served at home, even by very experienced cooks. *You* can serve it up in about 20 minutes. Here's how:

INGREDIENTS (for 4 people)

1 large barbecued duck (from your friendly neighborhood barbecue store) cut into 8 pieces by the barbecue man. You can use a chicken if absolutely necessary, but then call it Roast Chicken aux Fruits Flambé

½ jar orange marmalade

½ jar ginger conserve (marmalade), available in most stores, but if you have to substitute, use ½ jar damson plum jam and 1 teaspoon ground ginger instead

2 tablespoons teriyaki sauce

½ cup orange juice

1 cup cut-up peaches, or 1 cup orange sections or pitted cherries—fresh or canned

½ cup brandy

PROCEDURE

1. Turn on oven to 375° F.

2. Put the pieces of duck in the pan, skin side up.

3. Put all of the listed ingredients *except* the brandy into the saucepan. Now add just 2 tablespoons of the brandy and save the rest.

4. Bring the ingredients to a boil over low heat, stirring constantly.

5. As soon as the sauce begins to bubble, remove it from the stove. Spoon it over the duck, making sure that every piece is well covered.

6. Set the saucepan aside but don't wash it. Put the duck into the oven. Roast it for 20 minutes or until the sauce is bubbly and somewhat glazed. Don't worry about cooking a duck that is already cooked. Not only won't it hurt it—it's good for it!

7. Transfer the duck to a flameproof platter and spoon any extra sauce over it.

8. Pour the leftover brandy into the unwashed saucepan and bring it to a boil.

9. Take the duck to the table at once and pour the hot brandy over it. Then touch a match to it and get out of the way! It will burn with a high and handsome blue flame which finishes glazing the duck and the sauce. Just watch it and be amazed. You don't have to do anything. When all of the alcohol has burned up, the flame will go out by itself and the duck is ready to serve.

MEATS

MEAT LOAF

Nobody needs a cookbook to fry or broil a plain hamburger. But you can win fame and acclaim if you use the following gourmet mixture. Use it for hamburgers or meat balls too.

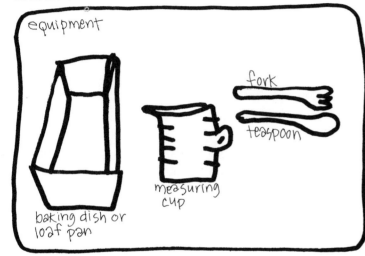

equipment

baking dish or loaf pan

measuring cup

fork

teaspoon

INGREDIENTS

1½ pounds chopped sirloin or round of beef

1 egg

½ package dehydrated onion soup mix

½ teaspoon salt

dash pepper

½ cup bread crumbs (for a spicier meat loaf—or for meat balls—use Italian flavored bread crumbs)

½ cup water

PROCEDURE

1. Turn on oven to 350° F.

2. Put all ingredients into the baking pan and mix them with a fork. If the going is too hard with a fork, use your hands.

3. When the ingredients are well blended, form a round loaf in a round or square pan, a loaf-shaped one in a loaf pan. When you pat the meat into shape, do it as lightly as possible. If you *pound* it into shape, the meat loaf will be compressed and hard. If you shape it gently, it will have a light and fluffy texture.

4. Bake, uncovered, for 1 hour.

VEAL PICCATA

Everyone should have some fantastic meat dish that can be whipped up and served with pride in ten minutes.

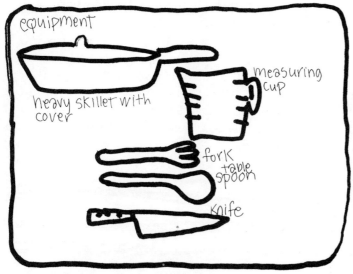

equipment

heavy skillet with cover

measuring cup

fork

table spoon

knife

INGREDIENTS (for 3–4 servings)

1 pound veal scallopini
a handful of flour
2 chicken bouillon cubes
¼ cup water
¼ cup dry white wine or dry vermouth
olive oil
salt and pepper
a lemon
fresh parsley

PROCEDURE

1. Spread out the meat on the butcher paper it came in. Sprinkle meat with salt and pepper and coat both sides with flour. After you have sprinkled flour on both sides of the meat, shake it off so that only a light coating remains.

2. Heat the skillet on top of the stove and pour in just enough olive oil to cover the bottom of the pan.

3. Put the veal into the pan and cook it over high heat for about 1 minute on each side or until it is lightly browned.

4. Turn the heat very low. Add the water and wine (or vermouth) and the chicken bouillon cubes. Mash the cubes with a fork and mix them into the liquid.

5. Cover the pan and cook for about 5 minutes or until the meat is so tender that you can easily cut it with a fork.

6. While you are waiting, cut the lemon into paper-thin slices and chop the parsley with a knife.

7. As soon as the meat is finished, spread the lemon slices over the top and cook for a few seconds longer.

8. Remove from stove, sprinkle with parsley and serve.

66

GLAZED BAKED HAM À L'ORANGE

This is one of those impressive affairs that could have taken all day to prepare. Only it didn't, because you started with an already-cooked canned ham and turned it into a gourmet triumph. Serve it hot or cold.

equipment

measuring cup

tablespoon

small bowl

large sharp knife

baking pan large enough to hold the ham

INGREDIENTS

a cooked canned ham—2, 3, 5 or more pounds. Quantities of other ingredients given are for a 3-pound ham which will serve 6–8 people.

1 orange
½ cup orange marmalade
½ cup brown sugar
2 tablespoons mustard
25 to 30 whole cloves

PROCEDURE

1. Remove the ham from the can (the hardest part of the procedure!) and pick off all the gelatin that is stuck to it.

2. Put the ham on the baking pan. Use a large sharp knife to make diagonal cuts across the top of the ham. The cuts should be about 1 inch apart and about ½ inch deep.

3. Now make the same kind of cuts in the other direction so that you form diamonds.

4. Stick one whole clove right in the center of each diamond.

5. Turn on the oven to 350° F.

6. Wash the orange, cut it in half, then slice one of the halves into 3 or 4 slices. Put the slices on top of the ham.

7. Squeeze the juice of the other half into a small bowl. Add the marmalade, sugar, and mustard. Mix it all together and spread about half of it over the top of the ham and orange slices.

8. Put the ham into the oven and bake it for about 1 hour. Every once in a while, dribble some more of the glaze mix over the top of the ham and let it run down the sides. If the glaze isn't shiny and brownish toward the end of the hour, turn up the heat to 400° F for a few minutes.

PERFECT POT ROAST

is another "cheat" recipe. It tastes like anybody's grand-mother's prize production, but it's so simple your little brother could make it.

INGREDIENTS (for 4–6 servings)

2 pounds brisket of beef, fat trimmed off (brisket makes the best pot roast there is, but if your butcher doesn't have it, ask him for the next best thing)
1 tablespoon butter
1 package dehydrated onion soup mix
salt and pepper
water

PROCEDURE

1. Turn on oven at 350° F.

2. Put pot on stove over high heat until the bottom is hot.

3. Add the butter and as soon as it melts and begins to brown, add the meat.

4. Sprinkle the meat with salt and pepper, turn it over with a fork and sprinkle the other side.

5. Turn down the heat about halfway so that the meat doesn't burn, but let it get well browned on both sides.

6. Add ¾ cup water and the onion soup. Stir.

7. Cover the pot and put it into the oven.

8. Roast the meat for about 2 hours, checking every once in a while to see if it needs water. The gravy should be thick, but of course you don't want the meat to burn—or the gravy to disappear altogether. If necessary, add more water, but never more than ½ cupful at a time.

9. It is impossible to give an exact cooking time for pot roast since it depends on the kind of meat, its shape and the kind of pan it's in. Stick a fork in it to find out when it is very, very tender. Start testing after 1½ hours.

10. When the meat is done, lift it out of the pot with a fork and put it on a cutting board. Slice it and arrange the slices in the gravy, then reheat.

11. You can do all that ahead of time if you like and just heat the pot roast again when you are ready to serve it. It is at its very best if you make it a day before you need it and refrigerate it overnight. This is especially useful if the meat is fatty. After refrigeration, the fat is in a solid cake on top of the gravy and you can just lift it off and throw it away. Reheat in the oven or on top of the stove.

BEEF STROGANOFF

Any main dish that can be prepared ahead of time and reheated is desirable for company dinners.

Ingredients (for 4 servings)

1½ pounds beef for Stroganoff (your butcher will pound slices of round steak until they are very thin, then cut them into strips about 2 inches long by ½ inch wide)

4 tablespoons flour

1 teaspoon salt

¼ teaspoon pepper

2 tablespoons ketchup

1 tablespoon Worcestershire sauce

1 teaspoon dry mustard (if you don't have any, use 2 teaspoons regular mustard)

2 beef bouillon cubes

½ pound fresh mushrooms (or 1 small can)

1 small (8-ounce) container sour cream

4 tablespoons (½ stick) butter

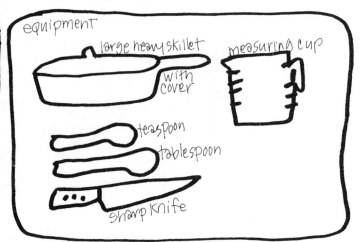

equipment

large heavy skillet with cover

measuring cup

teaspoon

tablespoon

sharp knife

PROCEDURE

1. Spread out the meat on the butcher paper. Sprinkle with the salt, pepper and flour and roll the meat around until every piece is coated on all sides.

2. Put the butter into the skillet and heat it on top of the stove until the butter begins to bubble. Drop in the meat and brown each piece on both sides. Lower heat to medium and watch to see that the meat doesn't burn.

3. Stir and turn it often until it is equally brown on all sides. Then add 1 cup of water and the bouillon cubes. As soon as the cubes have softened, mash them with the spoon and stir well.

4. Turn the heat as low as possible. Add the ketchup, Worcestershire sauce, and mustard. Cover the pan and cook for $1\frac{1}{4}$ hours. You will have to stir very often and add a little bit of water whenever the mixture looks dry or begins to stick to the pan. The sauce should be very thick, so be careful not to make it thin or watery.

5. After $1\frac{1}{4}$ hours, add the sliced mushrooms (or leave them whole if they are very small) and cook another 15 minutes. The meat should be so tender that you can easily cut it with the side of the spoon. If it isn't that tender, cook it longer.

6. When the meat is ready, you have reached the point where you can turn it off and wait or go ahead. Just before serving, add about $\frac{2}{3}$ of the container of sour cream and stir it until all the lumps are gone and the sauce is perfectly smooth. Heat the Stroganoff until it is very hot, stirring often, but do *not* let it boil once you have added the cream. Serve it over rice or noodles. Or kasha. Or couscous.

MALAYAN CURRY

This is an exotic way to use up leftover meat or poultry.

equipment

sharp knife

small bowl

measuring cup

large heavy skillet or Dutch oven with cover

strainer

tablespoon

cup

INGREDIENTS (to serve 4 or 5)

3 to 4 cups diced leftover beef, lamb, chicken or turkey
2 medium onions, chopped
2 tablespoons vegetable oil or butter
1 3½-ounce can flaked coconut
1 tablespoon curry powder
1¼ cups milk
1 tablespoon flour
4 tablespoons water
1 tablespoon lemon juice
about ½ tablespoon salt

PROCEDURE

1. Put the milk and coconut into the pan, stir, and boil very, very gently for about 2 minutes.

2. Put a strainer over a small bowl and pour the mixture into it. Use the back of a spoon to press as much of the milk out of the coconut as you can, then just leave it alone for a while.

3. Put the oil or butter into the pan and add the onions. Cook over medium heat, stirring occasionally, until the onions are golden.

4. Stir in the meat and curry and mix well. Cover and leave on low heat for about 10 minutes, stirring a few times.

5. Put the flour into a cup and add the water. Stir until perfectly smooth.

6. Add the flour mixture, salt, and the milk that is under the strainer to the meat pan. Taste it to see if it needs more salt, then bring it to a boil.

7. Stir until the sauce is smooth, then add the lemon juice and coconut and stir again.

8. Serve with brown or white rice and chutney (page 92). You can put out small dishes of raisins and chopped nuts as extra accompaniments if you choose.

VEGETABLES
& SALADS

Vegetables and salads are lumped together in this chapter because a salad can often take the place of a cooked vegetable. A large, varied green salad can easily replace a green vegetable instead of being served in *addition* to it; and a starchy salad, such as rice or bean salad, is a pleasant change from a cooked starch for a hot weather meal.

Let's begin with the simplest vegetable:

BAKED POTATOES IN FOIL

This isn't exactly a gourmet recipe, but it's a very useful one. The advantage to baking potatoes this way is that it is genuinely difficult to overcook them. Start these an hour before you need them when you are trying to make a meal "come out even," but in case something else takes much longer than you thought it would, you can let the potatoes bake for an extra half hour—or even longer. No one will ever know the difference.

INGREDIENTS

medium-size baking potatoes
butter

PROCEDURE

1. Set oven to 375° F.

2. Hold potatoes under cold running water and scrub them with a vegetable brush. The skins are good to eat, so make them clean.

3. Rub each potato with a little butter and wrap it in a piece of foil that covers it completely.

4. Bake the potatoes for an hour or more. They should feel very soft when you squeeze one with a potholder.

5. Remove them from the oven, cut a cross in the top of each potato (right through the foil) and squeeze the ends to make some potato pop up through the hole. Put a blob of butter on top.

BRAISED ENDIVE OR CELERY

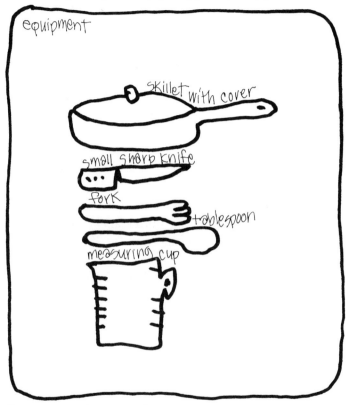

equipment

skillet with cover

small sharp knife

fork

tablespoon

measuring cup

INGREDIENTS (to serve 4)

4 endives or 4 large single stalks of celery
2 chicken bouillon cubes
2 tablespoons butter
½ cup water

PROCEDURE

1. Wash the vegetables in cold water. If you use celery, cut off the leaves and trim the bottom half inch from the wide end of the stalk.

2. Split endives into quarters, lengthwise. Cut celery into 3-inch sections. If the stalks are very wide, split them.

3. Melt the butter in the skillet and add the vegetables, water and bouillon cubes. Cook gently over medium heat, until the water begins to boil. Mash the bouillon cubes, stir them into the liquid and cover the pan.

4. Cook until all of the liquid is gone and the vegetables are just beginning to turn pale golden brown. Remove from heat at once.

GREEN BEANS GOURMET

To dress up the plain and simple bean.

equipment

medium-size saucepan with cover

tablespoon

measuring cup

INGREDIENTS (to serve 4)

1 pound green beans
4 tablespoons (½ stick) butter
½ cup blanched slivered almonds (buy them prepared)
salt and pepper
about 1 cup water

PROCEDURE

1. Wash the beans under cold water and break off the pointy ends.

2. Put the beans into the pan with the water and a dash of salt. Bring the water to a boil quickly, then turn down the heat. Cover the pan and boil the beans gently for about 10 to 15 minutes, or until they are just tender but still a trifle crisp. Bite one to find out.

3. Drain off the water and put the beans into a serving dish.

4. Put the butter into the pan you cooked the beans in and melt the butter over medium heat.

5. Add the almonds to the butter and cook them for about 1 minute, stirring often so that they don't burn.

6. Pour the butter and almonds over the beans. Sprinkle with salt and pepper, and stir.

CANDIED CARROTS

equipment

medium-size skillet

tablespoon

knife (for butter)

INGREDIENTS (to serve 3 or 4)

1 can baby carrots (the best ones come from Belgium)
4 tablespoons brown sugar
2 tablespoons butter (¼ stick)
cinnamon
nutmeg

PROCEDURE

1. Melt the butter in the skillet and add the brown sugar.
2. Stir constantly, over medium heat, until the sugar is dissolved.
3. Drain all of the liquid from the carrots and put them into the sauce. Cook gently, stirring occasionally, until the sauce is very thick—like molasses—and the carrots are well coated with it. Add a small sprinkle of cinnamon and nutmeg and serve.

GREEN SALAD

No meal is really complete without a good green salad. Make it as large or small, as simple or complex, as hearty or delicate as the meal, the ingredients available—and your own feelings—dictate.

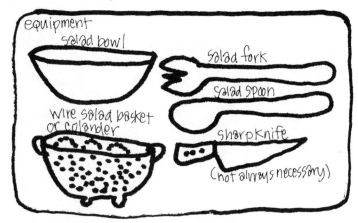

equipment
salad bowl
salad fork
salad spoon
wire salad basket or colander
sharp knife
(not always necessary)

INGREDIENTS

The possibilities are endless. Choose what you like—or what you can get. For basic greens choose from, or combine, Boston lettuce, romaine, salad bowl lettuce, buttercrunch lettuce, bronze lettuce—or just plain lettuce; raw spinach (which makes a great salad all by itself); watercress; arugala. Add avocado, parsley, endive, chicory (in small amounts—it's bitter), or whatever your greengrocer or garden offers. Add a touch of fresh (if possible) or dried tarragon, chives, thyme, oregano. Use your imagination. Be free and creative.

PROCEDURE

1. Wash greens and drain thoroughly in a wire basket or colander.

2. Shake out as much water as possible, then pat the greens dry with a towel.

3. Break up everything breakable into bite-size pieces. Use a knife for anything *un*breakable like avocado or endive.

4. Put it all into the salad bowl and leave it in the refrigerator until the last possible second.

5. Just at the moment of serving, pour a dressing (pp. 90–91) over it and toss well.

RICE SALAD

Here are a couple of hearty salads that are especially good for buffets or party food.

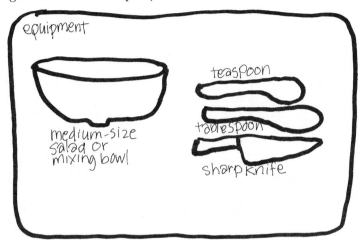

equipment

medium-size salad or mixing bowl

teaspoon

tablespoon

sharp knife

INGREDIENTS

2 cups cooked rice (p. 83)

3 ripe tomatoes, cut into chunks

1 large green pepper (or 2 small ones) cut into narrow strips

½ teaspoon salt

sprinkle of pepper (freshly ground if you have a pepper mill)

½ teaspoon dry mustard (or 1 rounded teaspoonful from a jar)

2 tablespoons olive oil

1 tablespoon vinegar (wine vinegar if you have it)

PROCEDURE

1. Mix all ingredients together in a bowl.

2. Refrigerate for at least 1 hour before serving.

3. Stir again at serving time.

MIXED BEAN SALAD

is one of the easiest salads of all, and yet it tastes—and looks—special enough to dress up a party buffet.

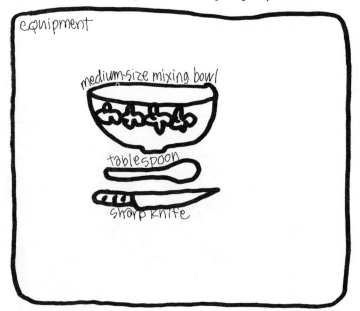

equipment

medium-size mixing bowl

tablespoon

sharp knife

INGREDIENTS

1 can cooked white beans
1 can cooked kidney beans
4 tablespoons olive oil
2 tablespoons vinegar
1 tablespoon finely chopped onion
1 tablespoon chopped parsley
salt and pepper to taste (about 1 teaspoon salt)

PROCEDURE

1. Drain the beans thoroughly.
2. Combine all ingredients in a bowl.
3. Chill for at least 1 hour before serving.

NOODLES
& OTHER
STARCHY THINGS

Noodles and pasta (spaghetti and macaroni products) come in all sizes and shapes. They are prepared by boiling them in salted water, and the directions for each kind are printed on the package.

Good tomato sauces for pasta are available ready-made, and recipes for the homemade variety can be found in most cookbooks. In the next chapter of this book you will find a recipe for White Clam Sauce which is splendid with spaghetti or linguini.

Noodles differ from pasta in that noodles contain eggs. The recipe that follows can be made with either fine or broad noodles. Try them both and see which one you like better.

NOODLES AU GRATIN

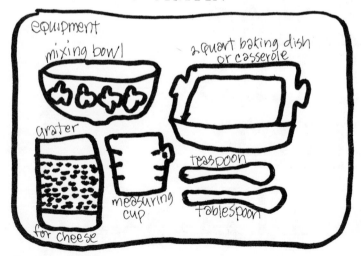

equipment
mixing bowl
2 quart baking dish or casserole
grater
measuring cup
teaspoon
tablespoon
for cheese

INGREDIENTS (for 4 servings)

½ pound noodles, boiled as directed on package, and drained
1 small container cottage cheese (1 cup)
1 small container sour cream (1 cup)
1 egg
1 cup grated Cheddar cheese
1 teaspoon salt
2 tablespoons butter

PROCEDURE

1. Turn on oven to 350° F.

2. Put hot, cooked noodles into bowl and mix 2 tablespoons butter with them until the butter is melted.

3. Grate the Cheddar cheese (unless you have bought it already grated) and set it aside.

4. Mix cottage cheese, sour cream, egg, and salt into the noodles. Stir well.

5. Pour the mixture into the baking dish and sprinkle the grated cheese over the top.

6. Bake uncovered for 30 to 40 minutes, or until the cheese on top is melted and beginning to brown.

BROWN RICE

If you aren't used to brown rice, you should be. It's better for you than white rice and it has infinitely more character.

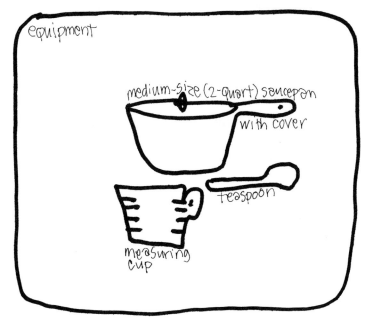

equipment

medium-size (2-quart) saucepan with cover

teaspoon

measuring cup

INGREDIENTS

1 cup brown rice

3 cups water

1 teaspoon salt

2 teaspoons butter (omit the butter if you are planning to serve a sauce or gravy over the rice)

PROCEDURE

1. Put the water and salt into the saucepan and bring it to a boil.

2. Add the rice at once and stir it until it begins to bubble again.

3. Turn the heat as low as possible and cover the pan tightly.

4. Cook for 45 minutes or until all of the water has been absorbed. Check occasionally during the last few minutes to make sure the rice doesn't burn. It is normal for some of the rice to stick to the bottom of the pan, but it shouldn't scorch. If the rice threatens to burn before it is tender, add a very small amount of water and stir. On the other hand, if the rice is cooked and there is still water in the pan, drain it off; then cook the rice for a minute or two uncovered, stirring often.

5. Mix in the butter and taste to see if there is enough salt.

MARIE'S HAWAIIAN RICE

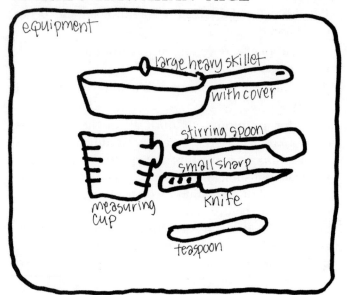

equipment

large heavy skillet with cover

stirring spoon

small sharp knife

measuring cup

teaspoon

INGREDIENTS

2 cups rice

4 cups water for white rice, or 6 cups for brown rice

¼ pound (1 stick) butter

1 medium onion, chopped

12 whole cloves

1 teaspoon cinnamon

¼ cup pine (or other) nuts

½ cup raisins or currants

1 small can pineapple chunks

1 teaspoon salt (or to taste)

PROCEDURE

1. Melt the butter in the skillet. Add the chopped onion and cook until the onion is yellow but not brown.

2. Add the raw rice and continue to cook, stirring constantly, for 5 minutes.

3. Add water, salt, and spices. Cover tightly and cook over very low heat until rice is done and water is absorbed (about 20 minutes for white rice, 45 for brown).

4. Add nuts, pineapple, and raisins or currants. Stir and serve.

SAUCES

WHITE CLAM SAUCE

For spaghetti or linguini.

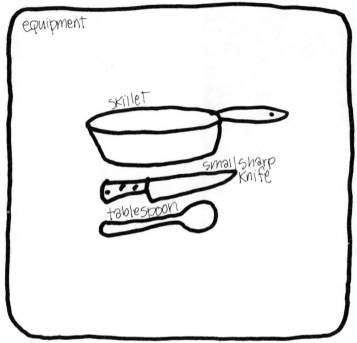

equipment

skillet

small sharp knife

tablespoon

1. Heat olive oil in skillet.

2. Add the chopped garlic. Cook it, stirring often, until garlic is golden brown. Watch it carefully because it goes from gold to black quickly.

3. Add all the other ingredients and bring the sauce to a boil.

4. Remove from heat at once and pour over hot cooked pasta.

INGREDIENTS

4 tablespoons olive oil
4 cloves garlic, cut into very fine bits
1 can minced clams
1 large handful washed chopped parsley
4 tablespoons butter
salt and pepper to taste

WHITE SAUCE

White sauce is one of those basic things that often turn up in recipes for all sorts of things. "They" just assume that you know how to make white sauce—so you might as well know. You can also use it just as is to make creamed anything—creamed peas, creamed carrots, corn, chipped beef—or as a sauce for fish or chicken dishes. Or mix cooked, diced, leftover anything with white sauce, sliced stuffed olives, salt and pepper and call it anything-à-la-king.

equipment

medium-size saucepan

measuring cup

teaspoon

tablespoon

INGREDIENTS

2 tablespoons butter
2 tablespoons flour
1 cup milk
1/4 teaspoon salt
dash pepper

PROCEDURE

1. Melt the butter in the saucepan and remove it from the heat.

2. Stir the flour into the butter and blend it until it is smooth.

3. Add the milk and seasonings and return to the stove. Cook the sauce over low heat, stirring constantly until the mixture thickens and comes to a boil.

CHEESE SAUCE

Follow the procedure for White Sauce. When you come to step 3, add ½ cup (or more, up to 1 cup) of grated Swiss or Cheddar cheese. Stir until the cheese is melted.

Cheese sauce is excellent on fish, chicken or a number of vegetables such as asparagus, broccoli, and zucchini squash.

WALNUT SAUCE

For a more exotic way to dress up hot or cold meat, fish or chicken.

INGREDIENTS

¼ cup chicken broth (you can use bouillon)
¼ cup bread crumbs
1 clove garlic
3 tablespoons olive oil
3 tablespoons lemon juice
¼ teaspoon salt
dash of pepper
1 cup shelled walnuts

PROCEDURE

Put everything into the blender and blend until fairly smooth.

GREEN SAUCE

is another means of turning almost any leftover into a masterpiece of exotica. Good on salad, leftover vegetables, cold meat, fish, or poultry.

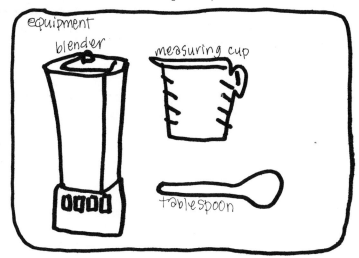

INGREDIENTS

½ cup white vinegar

1 cup olive oil

3 tablespoons bread crumbs

2 cups (about 1 average bunch) washed parsley with tough stems removed

1 tablespoon anchovy paste, or 3 anchovies

2 cloves garlic

3 tablespoons walnuts or pine nuts

1 tablespoon capers

PROCEDURE

1. Put everything into the blender and blend.
2. This recipe makes about 2½ cups. If it's more than you need, store some in a covered jar in the refrigerator.

VINAIGRETTE SAUCE

is *the* classic salad dressing and the only one you absolutely must know. Use it for green salad or any cold vegetable.

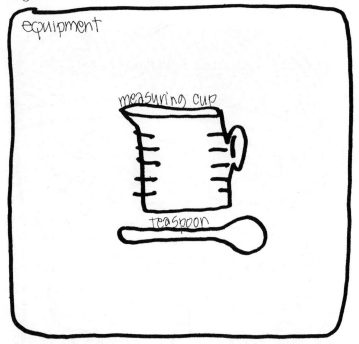

1. Fill the measuring cup to the ⅔ mark with oil.
2. Add vinegar until the 1 cup mark is reached.
3. Add the seasonings and stir briskly with the spoon.
4. This sauce must be stirred *immediately* before being poured over the salad. If you make it ahead of time, pour it into a jar with cover and shake it before you pour.

INGREDIENTS

⅔ cup olive oil
⅓ cup wine vinegar
1 teaspoon salt
¼ teaspoon pepper

ANCHOVY SALAD DRESSING

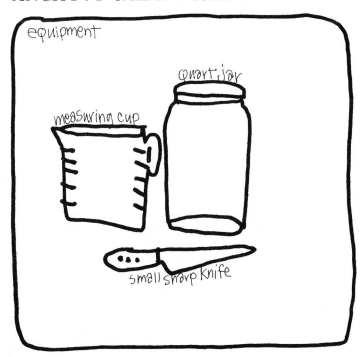

equipment

measuring cup

quart jar

small sharp knife

INGREDIENTS

¾ cup olive oil
⅓ cup wine vinegar
½ cup chopped parsley
½ cup diced tomato
6 anchovies, cut into bits
pepper and salt—if needed (anchovies are salty, so taste
the dressing before you decide)

Put everything into the jar and shake well. Best over a simple salad such as raw spinach or lettuce. Good on hard-cooked eggs, too.

CHUTNEY

This is a bit of trouble to prepare, but worth it. Serve it with ham, tongue, poultry, or anything that strikes your fancy. Chutney originated in India and is usually served with curries, like the one on page 72.

INGREDIENTS

2 cans (20 ounces each) crushed pineapple
1½ cups brown sugar
1½ cups cider vinegar
3 tablespoons finely chopped candied ginger
½ teaspoon garlic powder
1 tablespoon salt
1½ cups raisins
1 cup chopped walnuts or almonds
4 drops Tabasco sauce

PROCEDURE

1. Put all ingredients except raisins, nuts and Tabasco sauce into pot and bring to a boil.

2. Turn down the heat and cook gently for about 15 minutes.

3. Add the last three ingredients and continue to cook, uncovered, for 1 to 1½ hours—or until the mixture is as thick as jam and there is no liquid left floating around separately. Stir often.

4. Spoon the chutney into jars which have just been washed in hot water. Screw on the caps at once. When the chutney is cool, store it in the refrigerator.

THE BEST AND EASIEST CHOCOLATE SAUCE

This is classic over ice cream. Try it on pudding, too—or to make chocolate milk.

equipment

small saucepan

tablespoon

measuring cup

INGREDIENTS (to make about 1 cup)

2 ounces (squares) unsweetened cooking chocolate
1/3 cup water
1/2 cup sugar
few grains salt
3 tablespoons butter
1 capful vanilla

PROCEDURE

1. Put the water and chocolate into the saucepan and stir it over low heat until it is perfectly smooth.
2. Add the sugar and salt. Cook and stir for a few minutes—just until the sugar is melted.
3. Remove the pan from the heat and add the butter and vanilla. Stir until the butter is melted.
4. Serve warm or cold. Store leftover sauce in a covered jar in the refrigerator.

DESSERTS

One of the best desserts of all is fresh ripe fruit and a good soft cheese. But if your taste runs to sweeter things, here is an assortment for you.

CRÈME AU CHOCOLAT

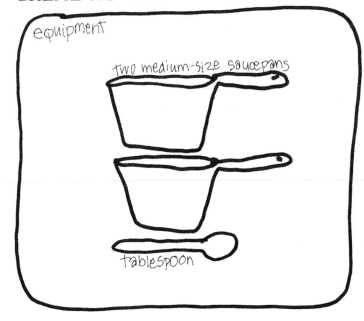

equipment

two medium-size saucepans

tablespoon

INGREDIENTS

2 cups milk
2 ounces (squares) unsweetened chocolate
4 tablespoons sugar
3 eggs
capful vanilla

PROCEDURE

1. Put the milk and the chocolate into bring it to a boil. Stir it frequent chocolate doesn't burn. When the m boil, turn off the heat.

2. Break the eggs into the second saucepan a sugar. Beat with a spoon until the mixtur blended.

3. *Very* slowly, a little at a time, pour the hot milk mixture into the eggs. Stir hard after each addition so that the eggs don't cook.

4. When all of the milk and chocolate have been added, put the pan on the lowest possible heat. Stir constantly until the mixture is thick enough to leave a coating on the spoon. Don't let it boil, because if you do, the *crème* will curdle. Should that calamity befall you, however, all is not lost; beat madly with an eggbeater until it is all smooth again. Needless to say, it's easier if you just don't let it boil in the first place. The whole cooking-stirring procedure should take about seven minutes.

5. Remove the *crème* from the stove and add the vanilla.

6. Pour at once into a bowl, individual dessert dishes, or *pôts-de-crème,* if you have them. Cover and refrigerate for several hours. This will be just as good if you make it the day before. Serve it plain or with whipped cream (page 16) .

...EN BANANA CREAM

equipment

medium-size mixing bowl

fork

measuring cup

INGREDIENTS

2 very ripe bananas
whipped cream (page 16)
½ cup sugar
½ lemon

96

PROCEDURE

1. Make the whipped cream and set it aside.

2. Mash the bananas in a mixing bowl with a fork. Beat in the sugar and squeeze in the juice of the lemon half.

3. Add the whipped cream and blend it all together with the fork.

4. Leave the mixture right in the bowl and put it into the freezer. Freeze it until it is firm but not hard. It should have the consistency of soft ice cream or firm custard. Note: You can make this with other fruits, too. Try peaches, apricots, or berries.

BAKED BANANAS

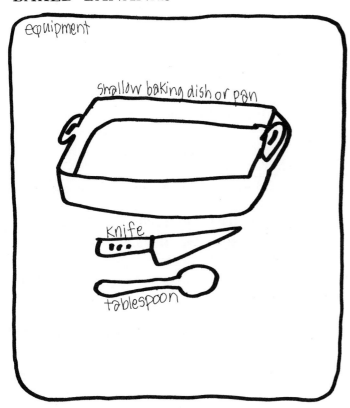

equipment

shallow baking dish or pan

knife

tablespoon

INGREDIENTS

4 peeled bananas
4 tablespoons butter
4 tablespoons brown sugar
½ lemon

PROCEDURE

1. Turn on oven at 350° F.
2. Butter baking dish.
3. Cut the bananas in half the long way and arrange them in the dish.
4. Sprinkle them with brown sugar and butter cut into little chunks. Dribble lemon juice all over the top of everything.
5. Bake for 10 minutes.
6. Spoon the sauce in the pan over the bananas until they are all coated with it. Bake for 5 minutes more. Serve cool or slightly warm.

APPLE CRUNCH

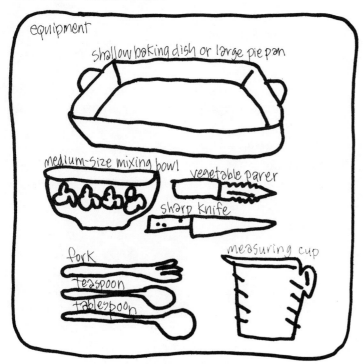

equipment

shallow baking dish or large pie pan

medium-size mixing bowl

vegetable parer

sharp knife

fork
teaspoon
tablespoon

measuring cup

INGREDIENTS

4 medium or 6 small apples
3 tablespoons white sugar
½ cup brown sugar
1 cup flour
½ cup (1 stick) butter
½ teaspoon cinnamon

PROCEDURE

1. Turn on oven to 400° F.
2. Break off a small piece of the butter and butter the inside of the baking dish.
3. Pare the apples.
4. Slice the apples by cutting off the four sides around the core, then cutting each of the four pieces into ¼-inch-thick slices. Put them into the baking dish.
5. Sprinkle the white sugar over the apples and mix it through.
6. Put the brown sugar, flour, butter, and cinnamon into the mixing bowl and mix it with your fingertips until it is well blended and crumbly.
7. Scatter the mixture over the top of the apples and pat it down slightly.
8. Put the pan into the oven. Bake for about ½ hour or until the apples feel tender when you stick them with a fork.
9. Serve warm or cool, plain or with milk, cream or ice cream.

LAZY CRÈME CARAMEL (LAZY FLAN)

The shortest route to a classic dessert:

equipment
medium-size saucepan
measuring cup
mixing bowl
fork
tablespoon
baking dish (about 8 inches in diameter)
a cake pan a little bigger than the dish.

INGREDIENTS

2 cups milk
4 tablespoons white sugar
3 eggs
capful vanilla
few grains salt
½ cup brown sugar (the granulated kind that pours)

PROCEDURE

1. Set oven to 350° F.

2. Put the milk into the saucepan and bring it to a boil. As soon as it begins to boil, take it off the stove.

3. Break the eggs into the mixing bowl and beat them for a minute or so with a fork.

4. Add the white sugar, vanilla, and salt.

5. Very, very gradually, add the hot milk to the egg mixture, stirring often. This isn't just hocus-pocus. If you pour the milk in fast, you will wind up with a bowlful of egg lumps!

6. Sprinkle the brown sugar in an even layer on the bottom of the baking dish and pour the custard on top of it. Pour slowly so that it doesn't stir up the sugar too much.

7. Set the baking dish in the cake pan and pour some hot water into the pan so that it is about 1 inch deep.

8. Move the whole works into the oven and bake it for 45 minutes. To see if the custard is done, stick a table knife into it. If the knife comes out clean, the custard is done. If the knife comes out wet and gooey, extend the baking time a little and try again.

9. Let the custard cool, then refrigerate it until it is really cold. At serving time, run a knife or spatula around the edges to loosen it from the dish. Invert a large plate or shallow bowl over the baking dish and flip it upside-down. The melted brown sugar will have formed a smooth golden sauce that pours over the top of the custard and runs down the sides.

CANDY

FAST FUDGE

is for those occasions when you are hit with the fudge munchies so urgently that you can't wait to make the conventional kind.

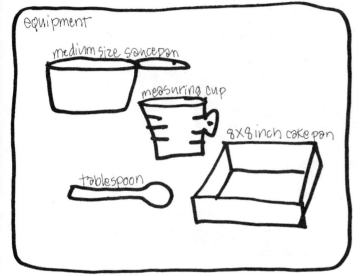

equipment
medium size saucepan
measuring cup
8×8 inch cake pan
tablespoon

INGREDIENTS

4 ounces (squares) unsweetened chocolate
1 tablespoon butter plus extra to butter pan
3 tablespoons heavy cream
capful vanilla
few grains of salt
1 egg
1 pound confectioner's (10-x) sugar
1 cup shelled walnuts or pecans, broken into pieces

PROCEDURE

1. Butter the pan and set it aside.
2. Melt the chocolate and butter over very low heat in a saucepan. Stir constantly to prevent burning.
3. Remove the pan from the stove and add the cream, vanilla, and salt.
4. Stir for a few minutes to cool, then beat in the egg.
5. Add the sugar and stir until it is all blended.
6. Add the nuts.
7. Press the mixture into the pan with your fingers and cut it into squares.

NUT BRITTLE

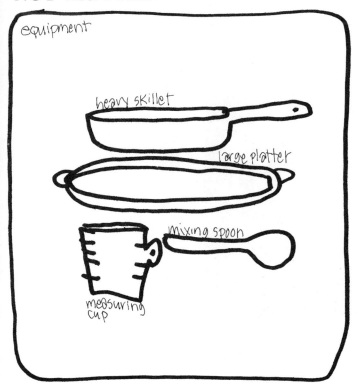

equipment

heavy skillet

large platter

mixing spoon

measuring cup

INGREDIENTS

2 cups sugar

1 cup shelled, unsalted nuts (whole or broken, all one
kind or a mixture)

few grains salt

a little butter to grease platter

PROCEDURE

1. Butter the platter.
2. Melt the sugar in the skillet over low heat, stirring constantly. After a while it will look like golden maple syrup with no sugar granules left at all.
3. Remove from stove at once and stir in the salt and nuts.
4. Mix well but quickly, and pour immediately onto platter.
5. When the brittle is cold, break it into pieces.

THE GOURMET
MENU-MAKER

The art of menu-making should not be overlooked by the gourmet cook. The best recipes in the world can cancel each other out if they are too similar: that is, if they lack variety of taste, texture, color, and flavor.

It goes without saying that a menu should provide adequate nutrition by its assortment of ingredients as well as its ability to fill stomachs. Even a totally inexperienced cook knows that potatoes, rice, and noodles do not make a good meal because they are all primarily starchy foods. But a surprising number of experienced cooks would not immediately be aware of the other serious defects in that menu; potatoes, rice, and noodles are all mushy, they are all bland in flavor and they are all more or less the same color. Horrors!

Although you may automatically avoid all of those pitfalls without even trying, here are a few sample menus just to help start you in the right direction.

LUNCH

Croque Monsieur
Green Salad

105

Green Salad mixed with slivers of ham and cheese
Anchovy Salad Dressing
Cream Cheese Biscuits

Quiche
Green Salad

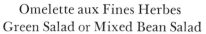

Lemon Soup
Hot Corn Bread

Omelette aux Fines Herbes
Green Salad or Mixed Bean Salad

Fondue Pudding
Green Salad

Any kind of cookies make a good lunch dessert. So does fresh fruit.

DINNER

Beef Stroganoff
Brown Rice
Green Salad
Banana Cream Freeze

Foiled Chicken
Candied Carrots
Braised Celery
Nutty Peach Pie

Sole Meunière
Green Beans Gourmet
Wheat Germ Biscuits
Crème au Chocolat

Broiled Shrimp
Marie's Hawaiian Rice
Green Salad
Galette Fruit Pie

Perfect Pickles
Linguini with White Clam Sauce
Cream Pie

Perfect Pot Roast
Baked Potatoes
Braised Endive
Lazy Flan

Cream of Walnut Soup
Oven-Fried Chicken
Braised Endive
Apple Crunch

Depending on your appetite, you can always add appetizers, soups, breads, and salad—where they aren't already included—to any menu.

May your appetite be hearty, and your cooking gourmet.

INDEX